Instant Persuasion

Instant
Persuasion

• • • • •

How to Change Your Words
to Change Your Life

Laurie Puhn, J.D.

JEREMY P. TARCHER / PENGUIN
A MEMBER OF PENGUIN GROUP (USA) INC.
NEW YORK

JEREMY P. TARCHER/PENGUIN
Published by the Penguin Group
www.penguin.com
Penguin Group (USA) Inc., 375 Hudson Street, New York, New York 10014, USA •
Penguin Group (Canada), 10 Alcorn Avenue, Toronto, Ontario, Canada M4V 3B2 (a division of Pearson
Penguin Canada Inc.) • Penguin Books Ltd, 80 Strand, London WC2R 0RL, England • Penguin Ireland,
25 St Stephen's Green, Dublin 2, Ireland (a division of Penguin Books Ltd) • Penguin Group (Australia),
250 Camberwell Road, Camberwell, Victoria 3124, Australia (a division of Pearson Australia Group Pty Ltd)
• Penguin Books India Pvt Ltd, 11 Community Centre, Panchsheel Park, New Delhi–110 017, India •
Penguin Group (NZ), Cnr Airborne and Rosedale Roads, Albany, Auckland 1310, New Zealand (a division
of Pearson New Zealand Ltd) • Penguin Books (South Africa) (Pty) Ltd, 24 Sturdee Avenue,
Rosebank, Johannesburg 2196, South Africa • Penguin Books Ltd, Registered Offices:
80 Strand, London WC2R 0RL, England

Most Tarcher/Penguin books are available at special quantity discounts for bulk purchase
for sales promotions, premiums, fund-raising, and educational needs. Special books or book
excerpts also can be created to fit specific needs. For details, write Penguin Group (USA) Inc.
Special Markets, 375 Hudson Street, New York, NY 10014.

Library of Congress Cataloging-in-Publication Data

Puhn, Laurie.
Instant persuasion : how to change your words to change your life / by Laurie Puhn.
p. cm.
ISBN 1-58542-323-8
1. Persuasion (Psychology). I. Title.
BF637.P4P84   2005   2004055363
153.8'52—dc22

Printed in the United States of America
1   3   5   7   9   10   8   6   4   2

This book is printed on acid-free paper. ∞

Book design by Lovedog Studio

*While the author has made every effort to provide accurate telephone numbers and Internet
addresses at the time of publication, neither the publisher nor the author assumes
any responsibility for errors, or for changes that occur after publication.*

With gratitude and love,
I dedicate this book to my mother, Ellen.

You have the vision to create,
the courage to try, and
the commitment to do.
You show me how one person
can make a difference in the lives of many.

Contents

Acknowledgments

I BELIEVE THAT all people are interconnected. When we give, we receive. Almost everything we accomplish is influenced by the presence of others in our lives. I could have had the most creative book idea, but without people on my side offering me their support and encouragement, this book would not exist. There are numerous people who listened to me talk about the Instant Persuasion concept. They believed in it, and because we had built a relationship based on trust and respect, they wanted to help me achieve my goals. They opened up doors for me and acted as mentors, infusing me with energy, self-confidence and knowledge.

Thank you to my former Harvard Law professor Alan M. Dershowitz. You believed in this book idea from its inception and encouraged me to carve out my very own path in life. Thank you to Monsignor Tom Hartman, co-host of the television show *The God Squad,* whom I met many years ago as one of twelve high school students selected to participate in "Project Understanding," an interfaith program. I am touched by your faith and confidence in me. By your example you inspire me to be a better person. Thank you, Rabbi Robert S. Widom of Temple Emanuel of Great Neck for showing me how to build bridges of tolerance and understanding in the world. I am deeply grateful to you for giving me an opportunity, at the early age of fifteen, to create programs designed to make a difference in the lives of others.

Much appreciation to my friend Greg Carr, former chairman of Prodigy and philanthropist, whose gift made possible the creation of the Carr Center for Human Rights at Harvard University. You are inspirational with your endless concern and compassion for others. Robin Wagner, who coached the figure-skating champions Sarah Hughes and Sasha Cohen, your energy and commitment made clear that a dream can become a reality. Thank you for sharing your thoughts with me. Much appreciation goes to Bernie Kaplan, principal of my alma mater Great Neck North High School. You are more than a high school principal; you are a constant guide, motivator and community leader. Our meaningful conversations have influenced my writing and outlook on life. To May Newburger, the former North Hempstead town supervisor, you are a politician with a deep sense of morality and conviction. Thank you for your encouragement. Lisa Comegna, director of events at Lord & Taylor, thank you for giving me the opportunity to launch the Lord & Taylor @ Night Series and spread the Instant Persuasion Method. Your warmth and friendly spirit made working with you a delight.

To Ralph Baxter, chairman and chief executive officer of the law firm Orrick, Herrington & Sutcliffe, LLP; Jeffrey Menkes, executive vice president and chief operating officer of Beth Israel Medical Center in New York City; Terry Burnham, author and Harvard Business School professor; Ariel Lublin, mediation coordinator at the Manhattan Midtown Community Court; and Dr. William A. Shine, former superintendent of the Great Neck Public Schools, your enthusiastic support is sincerely appreciated.

Thank you to Lisa Mettrock, president of the gourmet gift company A Tisket A Tasket Anything in a Basket, for sponsoring the innovative Six-Month Instant Persuasion Countdown Contest.

To my family, friends, colleagues, and especially my mediation clients whose words inspired the stories and rules in this book: Your verbal blunders and eloquent comments provided great starting points for the material in this book. All names and identifying details are changed to protect your privacy.

With love, I thank my parents, Ellen and Howard, and my sister, Jennifer, for their unconditional love and meaningful guidance. Mom, you taught me by example that success and values go hand in hand. I cannot thank you enough for sharing your wisdom with me over the years. The hard work and endless hours you spent reading and editing the manuscript will never be forgotten. Dad, your belief in the equality of men and women has positively influenced the way I see the world. Thank you for your kindness and unwavering support in believing that I could and should follow my passion. Jen, your creative talents and insight into human behavior heighten the quality of my writing and my life. Thank you for standing by my side and adding joy to each and every day as my caring friend and sister. With a deep sense of connection I remember my grandmother Frieda Vermut, whose love, devotion and words of wisdom travel with me every day. And to my ninety-one-year-old grandfather, Julius Vermut, who still reminds his grandchildren to "do what's proper," thank you for your kindness and generosity. I thank my grandmother Sydelle Prince, my uncle Al Vermut and aunt Nira Vermut for a lifetime of love and encouragement. I am grateful to have each of you in my life. Thank you to my cousin Sam Newborn for your guidance and legal advice.

To my wonderful and admirable childhood friends Dr. Anna Akerman, Alice Ku and Jason Menkes, thank you for your steadfast support, honest feedback and insightful perspectives on life. And to my former Harvard College roommates, who are an exceptional group of women—Nicole Agnew, Ilana Eisenstein, Jessica Kahan and Liz Peters—you always keep me on my toes! You, my dear friends, prove that saying the right words at the right time builds meaningful and lasting friendships. Faye Cumberbatch, Marian Tenenbein, Pat Bloomgarden, Jim Kaat and Richard Daily, your sincerity and kindness are greatly appreciated.

To my literary agent, Elaine Koster, I am eternally grateful. When you called me one Sunday afternoon and said three words, "I love it," you changed my life. Your wise editorial advice and commitment to this project are irreplaceable. Thank you to the enthusiastic team at Tarcher/Penguin, and especially to my publisher and editor, Joel Fotinos, who had the insight to recognize the importance of the Instant Persuasion

Method and help me bring it to life. To my editor, Terri Hennessy, thank you for your meaningful comments and valuable suggestions. I appreciate your commitment to this book. Your energy and spirit make me feel welcome at Tarcher. Thank you to my publicist, Katie Grinch, and to Kristen Giorgio, the marketing manager, for making Instant Persuasion shine. This is an exciting journey! I'm so glad that all of you are part of it.

Introduction

HAVE YOU EVER WONDERED why certain people have a ton of friends, a great job and a lasting marriage? Why they always seem to be successful at getting what they want? Maybe you think that they're smarter, work harder, were born richer or are simply luckier than you. Well, let me tell you a secret. It's not brilliance, hard work, wealth or luck that sets most successful people apart. It's their awareness and use of a power that everyone is born with but only some of us use—the power of persuasion. It's their ability to say the right thing at the right time in everyday conversations to influence people to like, listen to, cooperate with and respect them. Successful people know how to get what they want without spending a dime. They know how to pay with words of appreciation to get people on their side. They know how to use their power of persuasion to create rewarding win-win relationships based on mutual respect and appreciation.

Instant Persuasion™ is the quickest way for you to join the ranks of successful people. What is Instant Persuasion? It is an astonishing method of discovering, activating and using your power of persuasion in everyday conversations to win people over and get what you want from friends, family members and colleagues. The Method shows you how to avoid common communication blunders and employ communication wonders. The wonders persuade people to like, listen to, cooperate with and respect you so that people will help you get what you want in life. The Method relies on what I call the "people factor," because people are the barriers or carriers to your success. When you have people on your side, new opportunities open up to you. Through insightful stories you will learn the powerful Instant Persuasion communication wonders, which are the rules to use in everyday conversations. The ability to say the right thing at the right time empowers you with the skills to build strong relationships that lead to the things money can't buy: solid friendships, dates, a lasting marriage, the favors and the recognition you want from others. Instant Persuasion teaches you in minutes what most successful people know.

Although I first learned about the art of persuasion as a student at Harvard Law School, it didn't take long for me to realize that persuasion is not something that happens only in a courtroom. It happens in conversations everywhere, every day: at the dinner table with your spouse or partner, at your office with your colleagues and clients and on the telephone with your friends and relatives. Once you develop the mind-set that persuasion is an essential part of your everyday conversations, you will be able to use it to your advantage. With new information about persuasion, you will think differently and speak differently. You will attract people to you like bees to honey. You will get rid of thoughts such as, "I'm so unlucky," "I blew it again" and "Why doesn't anyone listen to me?" and replace them with "This is amazing," "I can't believe it worked!" and "This is too good to be true."

Instant Persuasion tells you what you're saying right and shows you how to quickly fix what you're saying wrong. The communication rules identify the simple comments you make to people every day in your personal, professional and social life that turn people on to you or turn people off to you. You will become empowered to speak with honesty, integrity and persuasiveness so that you never miss an opportunity to positively connect to people who will help you unlock the doors to your success. Whether you're disagreeing with someone, apologizing, gossiping, praising, listening, requesting something or giving or receiving criticism, there is a right and a wrong way to do it.

When you replace blunders with simple communication wonders, the words that work to resolve conflict, you will improve the quality of your friendships, deepen your relationships with family members and heighten your effectiveness at work so that people support you in getting what you want. The communication wonders are practical and solution-oriented. No analysis or interpretation is necessary. The communication wonders form the concrete Instant Persuasion rules, which are as easy to use as "Say this and you'll get that." Every time you use a rule, your personal connection to someone grows stronger and you open another door to getting what you want. *Instant Persuasion* is the handbook of rules that gives you the edge to succeed where others fail.

My discovery of the Instant Persuasion rules began when I was a student at Harvard College and Harvard Law School and continued to develop through my experiences and observations as a lawyer and professional mediator. As a board member of the Harvard Mediation Program, a former associate at the law firm Orrick, Herrington & Sutcliffe LLP and a certified court mediator in Massachusetts and New York, I studied mediation and spent a significant amount of time mediating legal disputes between neighbors, former friends, business owners and their customers, and family members. As a mediator, my goal was to facilitate communication between people to help them reach a satisfactory agreement and resolve their legal dispute without the intervention of a judge. Many times, a mediation would move along productively until one of the participants would open his mouth, put his foot right in it and throw the whole process off track. For example, I would hear antagonistic and disrespectful comments such as, "You're wrong," "That's a stupid thing to say," "You don't know what you're talking about" or "You should never have done that." Through my mediation experiences I repeatedly observed the astonishing power of words and how people can use words to instantly create resentment and conflict or support and cooperation. What many of us heard as children, "Sticks and stones may break my bones but names will never harm me," isn't true at all. What we choose to say to each other in the course of everyday conversations has a powerful connection to the quality of our relationships and the level of our success in life.

After noticing many of the same basic communication mistakes occurring over and over again in mediations, I knew there was a need for people to have better persuasive skills. The specific words people choose to say often have more influence on the outcome of the mediation process than does the content of what is being said. I began to view the mediation setting as a microcosm for real-world conversations. Over time I identified the most common communication mistakes, wrote them down in a journal and began to translate them into the Instant Persuasion communication blunders and wonders. Not only did I share my insights with friends, family members and colleagues, but I began to teach the Instant Persuasion blunders and wonders at seminars for men and women, young and old, in the professional, academic, business and personal growth fields. I received overwhelmingly positive feedback from seminar participants who contacted me afterward to tell me that the Instant Persuasion rules had changed their lives. Word began to spread about the power of Instant Persuasion, and I was invited to speak at more companies, community groups and professional associations. Responses to my Instant Persuasion seminars further validated what I already knew—that the rules work!

How can Instant Persuasion make such a monumental change in your life? Instant Persuasion recognizes the fact that common situations recur in our lives day after day. The situations don't change, only the people involved in them do. So the rules for dealing with these situations remain constant, predictable and reliable. You won't have to search for opportunities to use the rules because the situations will naturally pop up in your daily conversations. Instant Persuasion uncomplicates the complicated. You can learn the Instant Persuasion rules once and count on them for a lifetime.

Instant Persuasion is more than a set of communication rules. It is a way of life. While many people believe that success often comes at the expense of others, Instant Persuasion proves that the opposite is true. There are no trade-offs involved. Not only do you benefit from better relationships based on honesty, mutual respect and cooperation, but the people in your life will also benefit by having stronger, more productive and peaceful relationships with you. The more you use the Instant Persuasion rules to say the right thing at the right time to the right people, the more others will like, listen to, cooperate with and respect you. The more you connect with people, the more they want to support you and help you achieve your goals. Today is the day to activate your power of persuasion to change your words to change your life.

Instant Persuasion

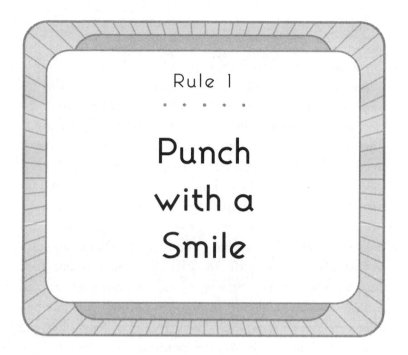

Rule 1

. . . . .

Punch with a Smile

HAVE YOU EVER HEARD the saying that a spoonful of sugar helps the medicine go down? Well, surprisingly that saying relates well to many of the conversations we have with others every day. Just as medicine tastes better when it is coated with something sweet, criticism sounds better when it is coated with sincere praise. A compliment given before a critical comment helps to sweeten your words and persuades others to listen to you and value your opinion. Some people may think this technique, which I call "punch with a smile," is heavy-handed, but it isn't, because the compliments that are given should always be truthful. There are plenty of complimentary things we could say to people every day but don't. Instead, we reserve praise for extraordinary accomplishments, or we don't praise at all because we think the person is already aware of what he's doing well. Too many of us are quick to criticize and slow to praise. Through the following stories, you will discover that the time to give criticism is also the right time to give praise.

On a Saturday evening, two friends, Tom and Jake, are at the movies. They have some time before the movie is scheduled to begin, so they head to the refreshment area to buy popcorn. Jake says, "You know, I almost had a date for tonight." Tom jokingly responds, "Too bad. Now you're stuck with me. Who was it with, anyway?" "It was with a woman I met last weekend at Starbucks. I stopped in to get a cup of coffee and I wanted to sit down for a few minutes, but there were no empty tables. So when I saw this attractive woman sitting alone at a table for two, I asked her if I could join her. She said it was fine, so I sat down. We talked for a while and she seemed nice, so I asked for her phone number. And believe it or not, she was happy to give it to me!"

"And then you called her to ask her out for tonight?" Tom questions. "Exactly," Jake replies. "I called her this morning to invite her to have dinner with me tonight, but she said she was busy. As a matter of fact, she didn't sound as friendly on the phone as she did at Starbucks, but maybe I caught her at a bad time." Tom asks, "Did you ask her for plans for next weekend?" "No, I didn't," Jake responds. "Do you think I should call her again for next weekend or wait a few weeks?"

Tom is definitely impressed by Jake's confidence and assertiveness in sitting down with this woman and asking her for her phone number, but he knows from his own dating experience that it wasn't a smart move for Jake to have waited to call her for a date on the same day he wanted to see her. So Tom says, "Actually, Jake, I do think you should call her again for a date, but this time call her earlier in the week to ask her out for the weekend. If you call someone for a date on the same day that you want to see her, chances are she'll be busy or even pretend to be because she won't want to seem so available. Besides, calling at the last minute might imply that you want to go out with her only because you have nothing better to do."

"Well," says Jake, "I don't like to make plans in advance. I wasn't sure what was happening this weekend until last night, so what else could I do?" "See, you just proved my point—you called her at the last minute because you were waiting to see if something better came up." Jake doesn't appreciate this comment and responds in anger, "Tom, what right do you have to judge my dating skills? Haven't you noticed that you're here with me, dateless, on a Saturday night?" Tom is put off by Jake's defensive remark and says, "I was only telling you what I thought. Would you rather I lie to you?" "No," says Jake, "but you don't have to be so critical. I only asked if you thought I should call her again." Tom doesn't want to start an argument, so he decides to keep quiet and instead fills his mouth with popcorn as they walk to their seats.

What Tom didn't realize was that he could have shared the truth in a different, more tactful manner that would have motivated Jake to listen to him and respect his opinion. When Jake asked Tom what he thought about the situation, Tom responded by telling Jake only what he did poorly. Tom didn't think about commenting on the positive aspects of Jake's actions. A better way for Tom to have handled this situation would have been for him to preface his critical comment with a sincere compliment. First he should have told Jake that he admired his confidence and assertiveness in sitting down with the woman at the coffee shop, getting her phone number, and calling her for a date. Then he could have offered his opinion as to what he thought his friend should have done differently. By sweetening his criticism, Tom would have persuaded Jake to be more receptive to his opinion without becoming defensive, and a rift in their relationship would have been avoided.

COMMUNICATION BLUNDER

It is a blunder to focus only
on what someone did wrong.

Sweeter criticism also has its place in the office. Notice how just a small change in words could have made Steve feel better about himself, his boss and his job. Steve is an investment banker. After recently graduating from business school, he went to work as an associate for one of the top investment banks headquartered in Manhattan. One day after lunch Steve returns to his office to find a note on his desk from Janet, the vice president of his group and also his boss. She wants him to stop by her office that afternoon.

Janet, Steve and the managing director who heads their group are all working on a presentation that they will give to a potential client later in the week. The client will compare their bank to other banks in search of the best one to help them raise capital to buy another company. Essentially, Steve's bank is part of what is commonly known as a "beauty contest," in which many banks compete against one another to offer the best proposal to land the client. Steve submitted a report to Janet the day before, which included a financial analysis of the client company along with some of his own creative strategies for ways to raise capital.

Steve has worked with Janet on other projects, but never before has he submitted an original report that contained so many of his own ideas. In the past, Janet seldom gave him any positive feedback, but Steve hopes that with this report Janet will recognize his abilities. He assumes that Janet wants to see him today to give him feedback on his report.

Steve walks over to her office and knocks on the door. "Come in," says Janet. "You wanted to see me?" asks Steve. "Yes, I read your report." Janet thinks Steve's report is very good, especially some of his strategies for raising capital. The first four sections of his report are quite impressive, but she thinks that section five is weak and needs improvement. As Steve stands before her in her office, she picks up his report and quickly thumbs through it until she gets to section five. She looks up at Steve and says, "I didn't understand your idea in this section."

She hands the report back to Steve and says, "Please revise section five for me by tomorrow. It needs more detail and clarity, especially at the end. Turn it in to my secretary when you're done." "Okay," says Steve as he stands there waiting for her to say something positive about the other sections in the report. But she picks up her telephone and starts dialing.

Steve realizes that she is finished talking to him, so he turns around and exits her office very disappointed. As he walks back to his desk he thinks to himself, "I put a lot of work into that report and all she did was tell me what was wrong with section five. Does that mean that the other sections are just mediocre? Now I can understand why so many people don't like working with her. Janet always looks for the bad things to say about everything. I'm not going to put more than ten minutes into revising the report. I think I've done enough already."

When Janet criticized Steve without giving him any praise she made a communication blunder that instantly persuaded Steve to resent her and resist her criticism. To Janet, feedback means telling someone what is wrong with what he did without telling him what is right. In this situation, Janet should have used the communication wonder to tell Steve that sections one through four of his report were quite impressive and well written *before* she made critical comments about section five. By first acknowledging what he did well, Janet would have motivated Steve to want to improve section five to make it as good as the other four sections.

Offering someone sincere praise before criticism is one way to persuade someone to listen to your opinion and motivate change without creating stress and conflict. Remember to punch with a smile and you will sweeten what could potentially be a sour situation.

COMMUNICATION WONDER

Punch with a Smile

Before you give someone criticism, whenever possible preface it with a sincere compliment.

Rule 2

· · · · ·

Spread Gossip

I KNOW A PERSON who always seems to find something bad to say about other people. It doesn't matter whose name pops up, she has negative gossip to share: "Have you seen Rachel lately? She and her husband are getting a divorce." "Did you hear about Tom's new job? I heard it was a demotion." "Did you hear what Jack said about you? He said that he thought you were rude because you left the meeting early." I must admit that at times I enjoy listening to a gossiper as she spreads bits of information that may be amusing or upsetting but are always revealing. Yet at the same time I don't trust her and I tend to keep a safe distance from her. I avoid telling her anything personal about my own life because I know that if I do,

I may be the topic of her next conversation. When I have a conversation with her, I find myself telling her that I have a perfect life, a great relationship and a wonderful job, even when that's not true. I deliberately tell her certain things, while I avoid saying other things in an effort to maintain control over what she says or doesn't say about me to others.

The truth is, this negative gossiper will never be my good friend. She will never be at the top of any guest list I make. But do you know who would be first on my guest list? It would be my friend who has positive things to say about other people and about me. Think about how you would feel about a person who tells you the good things that other people say about you. Wouldn't it be nice if she made a point of remembering to tell you that someone said how great you looked the other day or that someone said you had a fantastic idea at the committee meeting last week? Instead of keeping a distance from her, as you would from a negative gossiper, you would probably enjoy being close to the positive gossiper who passes on compliments.

So how can you become an effective positive gossiper? It's easy. If you follow the simple rule of spreading gossip you will quickly find daily opportunities to instantly persuade people to like you and appreciate you. The stories below will help you identify the many opportunities you have every day to spread positive gossip.

One day, as I told my friend Maggie the rule of positive gossip and described the amazing influence it has on people, her eyes grew wide and she exclaimed, "Wow, I can't believe how many times I've missed the chance to spread gossip. That rule of yours makes so much sense." Excited, Maggie continued, "Do you want to hear about something that happened to me last week that relates to spreading gossip?" "Sure, I'd like to hear it," I replied. And this is what she said:

One night, when I was having dinner with my friend Caroline, she told me that she was dating a guy named George, who, coincidentally, lives in my apartment building. She told me they'd been dating for about a month and she really likes him because he's so kind and thoughtful. Caroline asked me if I knew him. "Yes," I told her, "but not well. I don't often see him around the building. Although I do remember one time when he was especially helpful and went out of his way to carry some heavy packages up to my apartment." Caroline was pleased to hear my nice comments about George. Surprisingly, just a few days after my dinner with Caroline, I bumped into George by the mailboxes in my building. I smiled at him and he smiled back. "Hi, how are you doing?" I asked him. "Good," he said, and continued, "You know it's funny. We've both lived in this building for years and I think this is only the third time we've talked. By the way, do you know that I'm dating a friend of yours?" "You mean Caroline?" "Yes, I guess she told you. Well, she's terrific. I haven't met anyone like her in a long time. She's just a perfect mix of beauty and brains. I have such a good time with her." "Yes, she is a pretty amazing person," I agreed. By then I had finished getting my mail. I wished him good luck with his new relationship and headed up to my apartment.

Once there, I went through my mail and began to hang up some new pictures on the wall. I didn't think it was important to call Caroline to tell her the nice things George had said about her. I assumed she already knew that George liked her. The next time I saw Caroline I told her that I had bumped into George, but I didn't think to pass on his compliments. It's too bad. I realize now that if I had repeated what George said about her I would have made Caroline feel good about herself and more confident in her relationship with him. I also would have shown her that I wasn't jealous of her relationship, and she would have trusted that I wanted the best for her. Passing on positive gossip is a sure way to get people on my side. Next time I'll make it a priority to pass on compliments when I hear them.

COMMUNICATION BLUNDER

It is a blunder to keep compliments
about other people to yourself.

Spreading positive gossip takes nothing more than a moment of your time, yet it can make one of the most significant long-term improvements in any relationship. Now, let's see just how easy it is to spread positive gossip.

Jane and her colleague Maxine work in the same department at an advertising agency in Atlanta, Georgia. Everyone in the department knows that Maxine and the head of the department were involved in a very important presentation that morning in an effort to land a major account. Everyone hopes that they get the account because it would yield a significant amount of challenging new work for the department.

Later that afternoon, Jane walks over to Maxine's office to find out what happened at the presentation. She asks her, "How did everything go this morning? I'm dying to know." "It was fantastic," Maxine replies. "If we don't get the account, I'd be shocked. The many hours of preparation really paid off. The people from the company seemed to love our ideas and the creativity of our ad campaign. Our boss is a great sales-man. He really set an example for me. He was amazing at thinking on his feet and answering tough questions with total confidence and accuracy. Now we just have to wait a week or so until the company gets back to us with their final decision." "I'll keep my fingers crossed," says Jane. "But whatever hap-pens, congratulations on giving a great presentation." "Thanks," Maxine says. On the way back to her office, Jane walks past her boss's office. The door is open and he looks up at her. She smiles at him and he smiles back. For a split second she con-siders walking into his office to congratulate him on the pre-sentation and to tell him about the nice things Maxine said about him. But she doesn't want to be a gossip so she decides against it and continues down the hall. She figures he'll make a public announcement if they land the account and she can congratulate him then.

Did Jane do the right thing? No. Jane made a communica-tion blunder because she didn't recognize the difference be-tween a positive gossiper and a negative gossiper. While a negative gossiper destroys trust, a positive gossiper builds trust by showing others that she wants to make people feel good about themselves and she's happy for others when good things happen to them. By neglecting to pass on Maxine's compliments, Jane missed an opportunity to build a stronger relationship with her boss.

When she saw her boss sitting in his office, Jane should have used that moment to be a positive gossiper. She should have stopped in and congratulated him on what Maxine told her about his great presentation. She should then have gone on to repeat the specific compliments Maxine told her about him. If Jane had done that, she would have made her boss feel proud of himself and his accomplishments. Jane's kind words to her boss would instantly have persuaded him to like and trust her. In addition, her comments would have revealed to him that Maxine recognizes his excellent abilities, which would have made Maxine look good in his eyes. All in all, by spreading positive gossip Jane could have created a win-win situation for Maxine, their boss and herself.

The next time someone tells you something good about a person you know, think to yourself, "Aha! Here's a great opportunity to spread positive gossip!" Become a positive gossiper today, and tomorrow everyone will enjoy spending time with you!

COMMUNICATION WONDER

Spread Gossip

When someone tells you something good about a person you know, spread positive gossip by passing on the compliment to that person.

Rule 3

· · · · ·

Complain with Impact

WHY DOES SOMEONE COMPLAIN? He complains be-
cause he wants people to pay attention to him. He complains
because he wants something he doesn't have. He complains
because he sees a problem and he wants it fixed. Does complaining work? No, not really, because a person with a reputation as a "complainer" usually persuades others to ignore him,
dislike him and avoid him because he is annoying. Obviously,
it's not in anyone's best interest to be known as a complainer.
So how do you handle a situation in which it is both necessary
and appropriate to point out a problem and state your opinion? There are two ways to handle such a situation. There is
the wrong way: you act like a complainer and by doing so per-

suade people to ignore you; and there is the right way: you act like a problem-solver, which persuades people to cooperate with you. The amazing thing is that once you recognize the difference between a complainer and a problem-solver, you can easily transform yourself into a problem-solver and increase your chances of getting what you want. The key to this instant transformation can be found in the following stories.

Making a decision about where to go for dinner with the family can sometimes be an ordeal. However, this particular time it proved to be unusually annoying. Jason was home from college for his winter vacation and was spending a "family day" at his parents' house with some of the extended family. Everyone was joking around and enjoying one another's company, until they started talking about where to have dinner that night.

Jason's father, Bill, a meat lover, quickly said, "How about a steak restaurant?" "No, I don't feel like eating steak," Jason said without a moment's delay. "It's too heavy and I'm not that hungry." Bill wasn't happy with that answer because he wanted steak, so he pointed out, "Well, you don't have to eat steak at a steak restaurant. There is also seafood on the menu." "But I don't like seafood. You know I hate the smell of fish," Jason said. Bill rolled his eyes and took a deep breath, but before he could say anything else, Jason's uncle Seymour made another suggestion. "How about an Italian restaurant?" Bill wanted to end the conversation before he became annoyed with Jason, so he said, "Okay, fine. Let's go to an Italian restaurant." Everyone, even Jason, accepted the Italian option as well.

"Good," said Bill, "then Italian it is." But the conversation wasn't over. "Which Italian restaurant do you want to go to?" asked Jason. "You know, they're not all the same." Then Jason's mother, Helen, chimed in with a suggestion. "Let's go to the Italian restaurant in the shopping center near the house. It's close and I like the food there." But that didn't appeal to Jason. "It's too noisy there. I don't understand how anyone likes that restaurant."

Now Helen's patience was being tested, too. Everyone could see that Bill was leaning forward in his chair, frustrated and getting ready to attack Jason. "All right then, how about Giovanni's?" Helen suggested. "But we always go there. Can't we go someplace else this time?" exclaimed Jason. Now Bill had heard enough. He couldn't take any more of Jason's complaining. "Jason, you don't like anything!" he yelled. "Why don't you come up with a suggestion yourself instead of complaining about everything to everyone?" "Dad, why are you getting so angry?" Jason asked calmly. "It's just dinner." Bill answered, "Well, if it's just dinner, then stop being so picky. We're going to Giovanni's and that's it! If you don't want to come you can stay home."

What a pleasant family conversation! The discussion turned into an argument between Jason and his father because Jason complained about everyone's suggestions without offering one of his own. By the time they settled on Giovanni's, everyone in the room was annoyed with Jason for being so difficult and no longer cared what he thought.

This next story involves a complainer in the workplace. Marcy gets to work one Monday morning and sees a pile of orders on her desk in addition to the stack of orders she left in her in box on Friday. "No, not more work!" she thinks to herself. Marcy's job is to enter new orders into the computer system and manage the inventory for a small wholesale vitamin company that sells to retail stores. Marcy's colleague Julie, who also enters new orders and sets up the shipping schedule, is on vacation for two weeks. The day before Julie left for vacation, Marcy's supervisor told her he wanted her to take on Julie's workload while Julie was gone.

Upset, Marcy's mind starts to wander. "I still have work to do from last week. There is no way I can get everything done. The new orders will just have to wait until Julie comes back. So what if the shipments are delayed and the customers get upset? It's not my problem."

As the morning passes, Marcy gets more and more worried about the situation so she decides to tell her supervisor that it's impossible for her to cover for Julie and do her own job at the same time. She briskly walks to her supervisor's office and knocks on the door. "Come in," says Mr. Marshall. "Yes, Marcy, what is it?" he asks. Marcy answers, "I just want you to know that I will try to do as much work as I can this week, but there is absolutely no way I'll be able to handle my job and Julie's job successfully." Mr. Marshall doesn't understand the extent of the problem so he says, "Tell me what it is that you don't have time to do." "Well, I definitely can't get all the orders entered this week because I still have to finish entering last week's orders. As the number of orders increases, so does the amount of time I have to spend managing the inventory. I don't know how you expect me to get Julie's work done, too."

Mr. Marshall is instantly persuaded to dislike Marcy and resent her because of her negative attitude and complaint. He tells her, "It's company policy to enter every order on the day it arrives and then put it on the shipping schedule. We won't be able to manage the inventory if we don't do this." As he sees it, there is only one solution to the problem: "Marcy," he says, "there is no choice. You'll have to work overtime for the next two weeks to get all your work done." That is definitely not what Marcy wants to hear from him. She and her husband already made dinner plans with friends and purchased tickets for a show this week. Angry with her supervisor and also annoyed with her colleague for being on vacation, Marcy stomps out of her supervisor's office feeling more stressed out than she had all day.

Do you know what Marcy's communication blunder was? It's not that Marcy complained to her supervisor about her workload; it's that she walked into her supervisor's office without offering any possible solutions to her problem. As a result, she sounded like a complainer, focusing on the problem rather than the solution. Her boss was annoyed by her complaints, so to resolve the problem, he came up with a quick solution, one that did not appeal to Marcy.

If Marcy had taken the time to think through a viable solution to the problem before she complained to her boss, she might have gotten the result she wanted. For example, Marcy could have told her boss about the problem and then suggested that until Julie returned, she could make sure that the inventory was up to date for orders designated for immediate delivery. That way the customers would be happy and the company records would be in order. Or maybe another employee could help her out. If Marcy had come forward with a reasonable solution to her problem, she might not have been stuck with Mr. Marshall's first and only solution to her problem—that she work overtime.

COMMUNICATION BLUNDER

It is a blunder to complain about something without offering a solution.

As you can see, opening your mouth to complain about a problem without offering a solution can backfire on you and make matters worse. Now see what happens when Nancy complains to her husband, Jim. Nancy, who has been out in the rain for the last fifteen minutes walking her dog, returns home. Dressed in a raincoat, grasping her umbrella in one hand and the leash in the other, she pushes open the door with her foot. She steps into the kitchen and turns around to kick the door shut behind her. Nancy drops her umbrella, throws off her raincoat and bends down to dry off the dog with the towel she left on the counter before she went out. Finally, when the dog is dry enough, she unhooks the leash and sets him free to wander around the house.

She walks into the den, where her husband, Jim, looking dry, relaxed and very comfortable, is watching television in his cushioned chair. "Hi, honey," he says. "I just got home from work. It's raining pretty hard outside now, isn't it?" "Yes," Nancy snickers, "but why do you care, the rain doesn't seem to be bothering you one bit." "What do you mean by that?" Jim asks in an attempt to assess the situation, wondering what he did to tick off his wife. "Jim," she announces, "I just spent fifteen minutes out in the rain walking the dog while you were here relaxing. If you remember, you were the one who wanted the dog in the first place. You never even walk him anymore." "That's not true," answers Jim. "I walked him this morning!" "Oh, big deal," says Nancy, "that was the one and only time you walked him this entire week. I'm sick of that dog being my responsibility." "Nancy, what do you want me to do? I work longer hours than you do. You know there's nothing I can do about that."

Nancy hates it when Jim uses his "I work longer hours" defense for not taking on more responsibility at home. It always seems to her that Jim finds enough time to take care of the things that are important to him, like his car or watching football on TV. "Jim, you know what? Maybe I'll start working longer hours and then you'll have to walk the dog, buy the dog food and take him to the vet when he's sick. How about that!" "Nancy, don't start with me again. You're just overreacting." "I'm overreacting?" Nancy exclaims. "Maybe you're under-reacting! You're sitting there warm and dry watching television while I'm standing here cold and wet. I'm definitely not overreacting. But I will, very soon, if I keep on talking to you. Enjoy your TV show. I'm going upstairs to clean up before dinner." Nancy walks away more upset than she was before she walked in the door. She can't believe that he could be so difficult and inconsiderate.

Nancy did not get what she wanted, which was for Jim to share in the responsibility of taking care of their dog. Instead, when she complained to him, he defended himself and denied the problem, and they ended up in an argument without any positive results. Nancy made a communication blunder. She complained to Jim without presenting a single solution to the problem. Nancy expected Jim to offer a solution, but he wasn't motivated to do that because he was very happy with the way things were.

Nancy should have used the communication wonder to persuade Jim to cooperate with her to give her what she wanted. She should have presented her problem along with a possible solution at the same time. Nancy could have said something like, "Jim, up to now I've had the responsibility of taking care of the dog and I don't think it's fair. I'd like to make a specific plan to divide up the responsibilities. So, how about if I walk the dog Monday through Friday and you walk the dog on the weekends and also take care of buying the dog food and supplies?" Or Nancy might have suggested another solution, such as that she walk the dog at night and Jim walk the dog in the morning and they share the other responsibilities over the weekend. By offering solutions, Nancy would have taken control of the conversation and focused it on solving the problem rather than on the problem itself. Needless to say, putting forth a reasonable solution would have made it easier for Nancy and Jim to come to a resolution.

The next time you have a problem with someone or something, present the problem and a possible solution at the same time to reduce conflict and lead the discussion to a resolution. When people see you as a problem-solver, not a complainer, people will listen to you and you will get the results you want.

COMMUNICATION WONDER

Complain with Impact

Whenever you tell someone about a problem, be prepared to offer a solution to that problem at the same time.

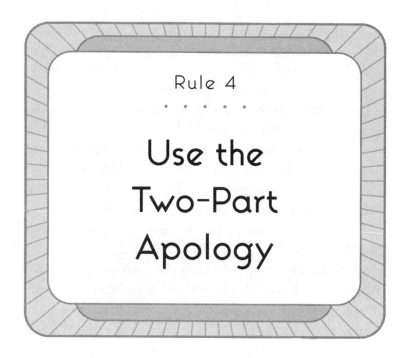

Rule 4

· · · · ·

Use the Two-Part Apology

YOU KNOW THAT YOU made a mistake and you want to apologize. But how do you say "I'm sorry" in a way that will persuade someone to forgive you? It is apparent to me from my professional experiences and observations as a court mediator that there are different kinds of apologies. Some are sincere, meaningful and satisfying. They help to put out the fire, reduce conflict and mend the relationship. Other apologies seem to be insincere, manipulative and unsatisfying. They add fuel to the fire and increase conflict. There are even times in personal relationships when someone says that she accepts an apology but then acts as if she doesn't. Why does this happen? Is there a way to get someone to fully accept your apology every time? The stories below will help you understand the difference between apologies that work and those that don't. Then you will learn the communication wonder to use to restore peace and harmony in your relationships.

Eve is sitting on the couch in the living room reading the newspaper when her husband, John, returns from an electronics store. He walks into the living room and tells her, "Guess what? I bought a large-screen TV just like the one we talked about a few months ago. Don't worry, it was on sale with free delivery, and the best thing is, it will be here in time for our Super Bowl party tomorrow." Eve is not worried about the delivery, she is very upset about the purchase.

She puts down the newspaper, looks at John and says, "How could you possibly forget that last week we agreed not to make any more big purchases, so we could save more money? We don't need a new TV. The one we have is working just fine." "But Eve," says John, "I know you'll love the TV when you see it. Anyway, there's nothing I can do about it now because it's being delivered this afternoon." "Yes, there is something you can do about it right now," yells Eve. "You can call the store and cancel the order!" "I can't," he replies. "I bought it at a close-out sale." Now Eve is fuming. "How could you decide to buy that TV without talking to me first?" she asks. "Hey," he responds, "it's just a TV, not a house. It's not such a big deal." John then realizes by the piercing look on his wife's face that he said the wrong thing. "What? We made an agreement and then you just ignore it and do what's good for you. I have nothing more to say. You're impossible!" Eve picks up the newspaper, gets up off the couch and walks into the kitchen.

Once Eve leaves the room and John has a moment to think about what he did, he starts to feel like it's possible that he made a mistake. After talking to Eve, he regrets his decision to buy the TV. He realizes he shouldn't have been so impulsive. He thinks, "I guess I did break our agreement. I should have talked to her before I put the money down. It is her money, too."

He wants Eve to know that he's sorry so he walks into the kitchen, where Eve is reading the newspaper and drinking a cup of coffee. "Eve," he says, "I'm sorry. I didn't mean to upset you." John stands there hoping Eve will accept his apology, but she doesn't. "It's too late," Eve says. "You just can't do something like that—say you're sorry and expect everything to be okay." John doesn't know what else to say so he leaves the kitchen and goes back into the living room to watch television by himself.

Eve didn't accept John's apology because she didn't think it was sincere. John suddenly did a complete about-face and apologized after defending what he had done. For all Eve knew, John still thought she was overreacting and the only reason he said "I'm sorry" was to end the argument. What Eve needed to hear, but John didn't say, was that he was apologizing because he had come to a real understanding that he broke their agreement and violated her trust. She wanted to know that he fully understood what he did wrong, so she could trust that he wouldn't make a similar mistake again. As you can see, John's simple statement, "I'm sorry," was a communication blunder.

*   *   *   *   *

COMMUNICATION BLUNDER

A blunder occurs when you only say "I'm sorry."

In the next story Mike and Leah will help you understand what works and what doesn't when you give someone an apology. Mike and Leah are friends and colleagues. They were both invited to their friend Wendy's wedding at a country club that is about forty-five minutes outside Chicago. Mike offered to pick Leah up at her apartment in the city at 5 P.M., one hour before the wedding is scheduled to begin. Once Leah has put the finishing touches on her makeup and selected the perfect jewelry to accessorize her dress, she sits down and waits for Mike to buzz her from downstairs. When 5 P.M. comes and goes, Leah becomes annoyed, but then reminds herself that their plan allowed for an extra fifteen minutes in case there was traffic. As long as Mike arrives in the next ten minutes, they won't be late for the wedding.

At 5:20 Leah can no longer reason her way out of being worried and upset with Mike for being late. He's been late for things before, but she thought that this time, because he knows she is relying on him, he would make it a point to be on time. "How stupid can I be?" she thinks. "I should have just taken the train no matter how inconvenient it is." Last week Leah asked the bride what time the ceremony was going to begin and she said at 6:10 sharp, after everyone had time for a glass of champagne. So Leah knows that if Mike doesn't arrive soon they could miss the ceremony. She continues to berate herself for relying on Mike to pick her up. Leah calls Mike on his cell phone to find out where he is, but he doesn't pick up her call.

It's now almost 5:30 and since Mike is nowhere to be found, Leah decides that she'll pay the extra money to take a taxi to the wedding. "I should make Mike pay for my taxi!" she thinks as she leaves her apartment. She is on the street looking for a cab when Mike pulls up. She walks to his car, opens the door and plops down in the front seat. "You're a half hour late! What happened?" she exclaims. Leah waits for Mike's response and wonders what his excuse will be this time. "I don't know. My suit looked wrinkled after I put it on, so I had to take it off and iron it, and then I couldn't find the right tie to wear with it. But we won't be late. I'll drive fast." "The wedding starts in a half hour. We are going to be late," Leah exclaims. "And please don't drive fast. I would like to arrive at the wedding in one piece! I can't believe you did this. I was already looking for a taxi when you pulled up. Don't you know how inconsiderate you are?" Mike calmly presses the accelerator, stares straight at the road and says, "I'm sorry."

Silently, they drive to the wedding as Leah decides that she will not rely on Mike ever again. She thinks, "He is completely unreliable and self-absorbed. He does everything on his own schedule and never thinks about anyone else." At the same time, Mike is thinking to himself, "I said I was sorry. What else can I do?"

Even though Mike said he was sorry, Leah still feels angry, unsatisfied and mistrustful of him. It is true that Mike's apology was a step in the right direction, but his apology didn't mend the situation because Leah isn't convinced that Mike was sincere. Mike blundered because his apology was hasty and incomplete. Leah has good reason to believe that nothing will change in the future because Mike probably gave her a quick apology just to shut her up and end the conversation.

What should Mike have said to Leah to persuade her that he was truly sorry? Mike needed to use the two-part apology. First, Mike should have acknowledged what he did wrong. He should have said, "I'm sorry for being late and upsetting you. I know you were depending on me and I messed up." Second, Mike should have specifically explained what he will do differently in the future to make sure that it won't happen again. "In the future, when I agree to meet you at a specific time, I won't be late. From now on I'll call you right before I leave my apartment to let you know I'm on my way." If Mike had given this two-part apology, Leah would have known that he truly understood what he did wrong and that he would make a sincere effort to avoid the mistake in the future. If, after hearing the two-part apology, Leah thought Mike still didn't understand what was upsetting her, then she would have had the opportunity to explain how she felt and how he was misunderstanding her view of the situation. When there is a conflict, a conversation that includes a two-part apology opens the door to a meaningful resolution.

The two-part apology is a communication wonder because it displays acknowledgment and regret and offers a detailed promise for a change in behavior in future. When you find that it's time to apologize to someone, use the following rule to find forgiveness and move your relationship forward.

•   •   •   •   •

COMMUNICATION WONDER

Use the Two-Part Apology

First, say, "I'm sorry for ____
[fill in with whatever you did wrong]."

Second, say, "In the future I will ____
[fill in with what you will do to prevent
yourself from doing it again]."

Rule 5

· · · · ·

Avoid Superficial Offers

DID YOU KNOW THAT there is such a thing as being too nice? Did you know that being too nice can create resentment and distance in a relationship? How is this possible? Well, your natural desire to be liked may lead you to make superficial offers. Before you know it, you have opened your mouth and made an offer that you don't really mean. You hope your friend will turn it down, but she doesn't. You become upset with yourself for making the offer. You think about taking back your offer, but if you do, your friend will resent and dislike you. So instead, you decide to follow through on your offer and you end up resenting and disliking your friend because you believe she has taken advantage of you. Ironically, your effort to pull this friend closer to you only served to push you and your friend further apart. In the following stories you will see how superficial offers wreak havoc on a relationship. Then you will learn how to avoid making those generous, yet harmful, offers.

After dinner one Wednesday night Arlene, her husband and their two children are clearing the dinner table when the telephone rings. Arlene is closest to the phone so she picks it up. It's her mother-in-law, Doris, calling to say hello. "Hi, Arlene, how are you doing?" "Good, we're just finishing dinner, so you picked a good time to call. How's everything going with you?" Arlene asks. "Everything's fine. I went to the supermarket today to buy some food for my July Fourth barbecue. I also ordered some platters of food from the deli. I'm really looking forward to Friday night. I think it's going to be a lot of fun celebrating Independence Day with the whole family, especially since we'll be able to see fireworks from the park near my house." "It will be nice. Zachary learned about Independence Day in school today and he was so cute when he tried to teach me all about the history of the day." Doris chuckled and said, "Maybe I'll ask him to teach everyone about the day when he comes over. You know, we're going to be about twenty people in all, with the family and my friends. I'm glad I have another refrigerator in the basement because I have so much food." "Really?" says Arlene. She already planned to bring something to her mother-in-law's house for the barbecue, a store-bought lemon pie that she knows her husband and her mother-in-law love. But now that she's on the phone with Doris, Arlene thinks, "I'll be nice and ask her if there's anything she wants me to bring. She'll probably say 'No, don't bother,' and then I'll tell her that I'm bringing the lemon pie for dessert."

So Arlene offers, "Doris, do you want me to bring anything?" "Yes, can you bring a big bowl of fruit salad?" Arlene is startled by that answer. It is not what she expected. "A fruit salad?" she repeats to Doris. In a flash Arlene assesses the situation and realizes that she doesn't have enough fruit in her refrigerator so she'll have to make a special trip to the supermarket after work to buy the fruit. Then she'll have to spend even more time cutting it up. Arlene can't believe that her mother-in-law, who knows that she works all day, could be so inconsiderate as to ask her to make a fruit salad when she could just as easily have ordered one with the other platters of food. Arlene wants to say, "No, I don't have time to make a fruit salad," but she can't bring herself to say that when her mother-in-law is being so nice by inviting everyone over for the barbecue. So Arlene says, "Okay, I'll bring a fruit salad." "Good. I really appreciate it. By the way, please put some blueberries in it. I love them. And try to make it really big. Fruit is the most popular dessert nowadays. Almost everyone I know is dieting." Now Arlene is fuming from all of her mother-in-law's requests. "Okay," says Arlene, "I'll put blueberries in the salad, as long as I can find them in the supermarket." Arlene has lost interest in the barbecue. She is irritated with Doris for dumping this work on her and wants to get off the phone before she asks her to do something else. "Doris, I have to finish cleaning up the kitchen. We'll see you on Friday. Bye."

When Arlene hangs up the phone she is angry with herself for opening her stupid mouth to make the offer, and she is just as upset with her mother-in-law for taking her up on the offer. "My mother-in-law has so much nerve to ask me to do this," Arlene thinks to herself. "If I was in her position I would never ask someone to bring a fruit salad for twenty people, especially if I knew the person was really busy. I would have made the fruit salad myself, or ordered it or just not served it at all, rather than make someone else prepare it."

Arlene blames Doris for this upsetting situation, but the truth is Arlene made a communication blunder and set herself up for disaster when she made an offer that she didn't mean. Arlene knew she didn't have the time or the interest to prepare anything for the barbecue. She had already decided to bring a store-bought pie, yet she foolishly made a superficial offer when she opened her mouth to ask her mother-in-law the open-ended question "Do you want me to bring anything?"

COMMUNICATION BLUNDER

Offering to do something you do not
really want to do is a blunder.

Expecting someone to know whether your offer is real or superficial only sets you up for disappointment and weakens the relationship. In the following conversation between two friends, Bonnie and Lynn, we explore how Bonnie's superficial offer harms their friendship. Then we will examine the communication wonder that Bonnie should have used to avoid the problem.

Bonnie is at home one Saturday afternoon reading a magazine when she gets a phone call from her friend Lynn, whom she hasn't spoken to in a few weeks. Bonnie, Lynn and their husbands used to have plans at least once a month, but they haven't spent as much time together in the past year since

Lynn had her first child. "Hi, Bonnie, how are you doing?" asks Lynn. "Good," says Bonnie. "So how's the baby?" "She's not such a baby anymore. Samantha is already thirteen months old. She's walking and talking and her vocabulary is getting bigger by the day. You have got to see her. So, how's your job going?" "Pretty good," says Bonnie, "but I am so glad it's the weekend! I'm totally exhausted from work. I worked from nine to nine every day this week. Tom and I are going to act like hermits this weekend because we're both so tired. We're ordering in tonight and watching a movie. But you know what, I'm sick of thinking about work. Let's talk about when we're going to get together. I miss hanging out with you. Maybe the four of us can go out to dinner one night soon?" "I'd love to," says Lynn. "But it's so hard to find a reliable baby-sitter. In fact, we have dinner plans tonight with some of Jeff's colleagues, and I was really looking forward to meeting them, but we can't go because our baby-sitter just canceled."

Bonnie, trying to be nice, instinctively offers, "Lynn, do you want us to baby-sit for Samantha tonight?" Bonnie is sure Lynn's answer will be no, especially since she just finished telling her how she was staying home that evening to recover from her stressful week at work. But Lynn is eager to find a solution to her problem so she immediately says, "Oh, you're a lifesaver. That would be great." Lynn had no intention of asking Bonnie and her husband to baby-sit, but now that Bonnie offered, it seems like a terrific idea. "Can I drop her off at seven? We have a reservation at seven-thirty." "I guess so," says Bonnie, who is surprised and upset that Lynn accepted her offer. "You're not going to be out late, are you?" "Oh no, expect us to be back by eleven." As Lynn says this, Bonnie is imagining her quiet, pleasurable evening turning into an exhausting night of listening to a crying baby. Bonnie is upset with herself for putting her foot in her mouth, but she's even more irritated with Lynn for inconsiderately accepting her offer when Lynn is aware of how tired she is. Bonnie knows she would never have imposed on Lynn in this way if the situation were reversed.

When Bonnie hangs up the phone she dreads telling her husband about the plans she just made for them for the evening. When he arrives home an hour later, Bonnie tells him what happened and he says, "I can't believe you offered to baby-sit. How could you offer that without talking to me first? I'm not in the mood to baby-sit tonight. Didn't we agree to stay home and relax?" His comments make Bonnie even more annoyed with Lynn. "Yes, we did, but I never thought Lynn would take me up on my offer. I expected her to be more considerate knowing my circumstances, but I guess I was wrong." Now Bonnie is so upset that she wants to call Lynn back to tell her that she can't baby-sit, but she knows that Lynn and her husband are depending on her and she doesn't want to be responsible for ruining their evening. Bonnie is stuck with the situation. She blames herself for making the offer and blames Lynn for being self-centered and taking advantage of her.

What happened here? Bonnie's superficial offer caused a relationship dilemma. She made a blunder because she offered to baby-sit when she didn't want to. Bonnie expected Lynn to read her mind and say, "No, but thank you for offering." Unfortunately, that didn't happen because Lynn took Bonnie's offer at face value and accepted it. By making that superficial offer Bonnie started a chain reaction that led her to become angry with Lynn and herself and caused her husband to become angry with her.

How could Bonnie have prevented this communication blunder? She should have expected her offer to be accepted. Since she was hoping that Lynn would reject it, she shouldn't have made it at all. If Bonnie had only followed the simple rule below, she wouldn't have ended up resenting Lynn, nor would she have upset herself and her husband.

The next time an idea for an offer starts to form in your head, stop, think and use the rule below to prevent yourself from starting a chain of events that creates negative feelings and weakens your relationships.

COMMUNICATION WONDER

Avoid Superficial Offers

Always expect a person to say yes to an offer you make. If you're hoping she won't, then don't make the offer.

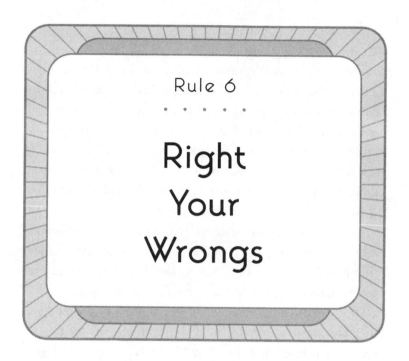

Rule 6

· · · · ·

Right
Your
Wrongs

WHY IS IT SO hard to say, "I'm wrong"? Why is it equally hard to say, "I don't know the answer"? Are we afraid that people will think we are unintelligent or incompetent? Are we concerned that people will think less of us? Well, for the most part, we avoid saying those seemingly self-deprecating words because we want to project a positive image to others. We want to appear confident, strong and knowledgeable. We want to look good in front of our friends, family members and colleagues. To do this, we may claim to know things that we don't know, or we may steadfastly defend a position we've taken even after we have been proven wrong.

Now, let me ask you a question. Do you think it's possible that by admitting you're wrong or you don't know something, you can actually make yourself look good? Well, interestingly, you can. When you say "I'm wrong" or "I don't know," you instantly let other people know that you are an honest person, confident in your abilities and open to showing your imperfections. Everyone knows that no one is right all the time so your willingness to say that you don't know something or to admit that you're wrong reminds people that you are a normal human being. In the next two stories you will see how pretending to know information or denying your error is a communication blunder that displays poor character and lessens the respect other people have for you. Then you will learn the communication wonder that helps you project a positive image.

Two friends, Dennis and Mitch, stopped at a diner one Saturday morning to have breakfast on their way to the golf course. Both men had low handicaps and enjoyed playing golf together. But their friendship never went beyond the golf course to social dates because Dennis and his wife found Mitch to be self-centered and his know-it-all attitude could be extremely frustrating. On this particular morning, Dennis and Mitch ordered their usual bagels and coffee and chatted about the week's current events. "Did you hear the news about how San Francisco city authorities are issuing marriage licenses to same-sex couples?" asked Dennis. "Yes," replied Mitch, "but you've got the location wrong. I think it was in Los Angeles, not San Francisco." "No, I'm sure it was San Francisco," said Dennis. "I heard it on the news last night." Mitch could not handle being told he was wrong so even though he wasn't sure he was right, he defensively insisted, "Dennis, I'm not wrong. You are. I heard it on the radio this morning on my way here. It was definitely Los Angeles." Dennis couldn't understand why Mitch always talked as though he knew everything.

Irritated with Mitch's predictable arrogance, Dennis thought of an easy way to end their disagreement and prove to Mitch that he was undeniably wrong. "I'll be right back," Dennis said, and got up and walked directly to the cash register to pick up *The New York Times*. He returned with the newspaper, moved his bagel and coffee aside and confidently spread out the paper on the table. "Look," he said, pointing to page three. "'Gays Marry in San Francisco.' Read the headline yourself." Dennis knew he had proved his point. Dennis wanted Mitch to admit that he was wrong, but Mitch wouldn't do that. "Well," said Mitch, who leaned forward to take a closer look at the article, "I thought I heard 'Los Angeles' on the radio. Does it really matter anyway?" Dennis was amazed at Mitch's comment. Even with the article staring him in the face, Mitch couldn't admit that he was wrong. Dennis realized that he should have expected Mitch to respond this way. He knew from prior experiences that he couldn't trust Mitch's statements because Mitch consistently preferred to be falsely right rather than honestly wrong. This annoying trait of Mitch's was exactly the reason Dennis wasn't interested in socializing with him.

Mitch made a communication blunder that turned Dennis off when he wouldn't admit that he was wrong. Mitch's words revealed his character—that he is a know-it-all who's untrustworthy. What Mitch proved was that he lacked the awareness that admitting he was wrong would not mean that he was unintelligent and insecure, but rather that he was intelligent and confident. Mitch's comments in the restaurant irritated

Dennis and reminded him that the time they spent playing golf together was more than enough.

COMMUNICATION BLUNDER

It is a blunder to say that you know something when you are not absolutely sure that you do.

Here is another situation in which offering inaccurate information and denying one's error creates mistrust and distance in a relationship. My friend Stacey came to me for legal advice after she had made the mistake of relying on some information she received from her uncle Henry. Stacey used to work for a large interior design firm. After five years at the firm, which included a few promotions, she decided the time was right to leave the firm to head full force into starting her own company. She decided to begin by working alone in a home business to keep the overhead expenses as low as possible. She also decided to create innovative business cards with her company name on them to attract customers. But Stacey wasn't sure what name to use for her company and how to structure the company legally. For that information, she immediately went to her uncle Henry for advice because he owned a very successful furniture company and she thought he was familiar with the world of interior design. "Uncle Henry," she asked, "I want to name my company something that sounds professional, like Stacey Jones Associates, but since I'm the only employee, is it okay for me to use the word 'associates' even though it implies that there is more than one person with the company? And do I have to register the name somewhere?" Uncle Henry had accumulated much knowledge over his thirty-plus years of experience in the business world and had become a very confident man who enjoyed imparting his knowledge to others. He knew he wasn't 100 percent certain of the legal answer to her question, but without a moment's delay, he said to Stacey, "It's fine to use the name Stacey Jones Associates. In fact, I like that name for your business. There are no limitations, although eventually you should register the name of your company at the New York City clerk's office." He told her, "Go to the clerk's office, ask for a 'doing business' legal form and then submit it to the clerk. You shouldn't have any problems." "Thanks for the information," responded Stacey, who was pleased to hear that the process would be so easy.

Within a couple of weeks, Stacey had designed and printed her business cards, along with flyers and invoices with the company name, Stacey Jones Associates, on them. She made lots of phone calls and dropped off cards and flyers at various furniture, carpet and hardware stores, as well as at local community centers. She knew that if her company was going to be successful she had to drum up business fast, and that publicizing her company on this printed material was a good way to attract customers. Sure enough, about a month later, Stacey's new business showed definite signs of success. Many people called to find out more about her services. When she explained her company's strengths—quality, price control and speed—people were eager to make appointments. Proud of her accomplishments, Stacy decided to run down to the clerk's office to register her company. She picked up the "doing business" form as her uncle had suggested, filled it out and had it notarized at a nearby bank. Then she returned to the clerk's office and handed in the completed form.

The clerk quickly looked over the form and then just as quickly looked up at Stacey and said, "I see that you checked the box for 'sole proprietorship.' Does that mean you are the only owner of your company?" "Yes," Stacey responded eagerly, proud of herself for having the motivation to start her own business. "I work for myself." "Well then," the clerk responded matter-of-factly, "you can't use the word 'associates' in the name of your business. It's New York State law. The word 'associates' can only be used when there is more than one owner. You'll have to use a different name. Take your form back." "What?" Stacey exclaimed. "This can't be. I already printed business cards and flyers with that name and I gave them out all over. I have clients! How can I suddenly change my business name without it looking suspicious?" "Well, I'm sorry," the clerk responded, "but I can't change the law. You have no choice but to change your company name. Look, you don't have to take my word for it. Here's a copy of the law. Read it and I also suggest that you take this blank 'doing business' form with you when you leave." Stacey left the clerk's office with the law in one hand and the blank "doing business" form in the other. She was angry with her uncle for giving her the wrong information but even more upset with herself for trusting him.

Stacey told me that she went home and immediately called her uncle to tell him what had happened. "Why did you say that I could use the word 'associates' in my company name when you didn't know the details of the law?" Her uncle defensively responded, "Well, I was pretty sure I was right. It just seemed like the logical answer to your question. I

work with companies of all sizes that have the word 'associates' in their name, so I just assumed that there wasn't any
legal limitation to the word and you could use it, too." "But
you never looked up the law, did you? You didn't know the
answer when you said you did." "Well, I never checked the
law, I just told you what I thought made sense." "Uncle Henry,
do you realize that I've wasted money on business cards and
flyers and I've spent hours going places to drop them off?
I've met with potential clients who think my company is
called Stacey Jones Associates. It's going to look unprofessional for me to suddenly change the company name. That's
no way to start up a business. I can't believe you put me in
a position like this."

"Look, Stacey," responded Uncle Henry, who didn't like being told that he was wrong or listening to his niece's unappre-
ciative attitude, "maybe I should have told you that I didn't
know the answer with absolute certainty, but I honestly think
that even if you're right about the law you're overreacting to
this whole situation. Just pick another name and fill out another form." Now Stacey was furious with her uncle. Not only
had he given her the wrong information but he continued to
stick to his position rather than admit his error and apologize
to her for the problem he created. Stacey hadn't realized, until then, that her uncle was such an arrogant man.

Stacey's uncle made a communication blunder when he
told her it was okay to use the word "associates" in the name
of her company, even though his answer was based on an assumption, not a fact. Stacey relied on his incorrect advice and
learned a lesson—never trust Uncle Henry's advice again.
Why did her uncle Henry make an assumption about the law?
Simply because he was usually right about things and he just

assumed that he was right about this, too. Unfortunately, his overly confident attitude placed his niece in an uncomfortable and unprofessional situation. This unnerving experience forced Stacey to take a second look at her uncle Henry and what kind of man he really was.

What should her uncle have done? He should have checked the facts before he told Stacey what to do. He should have used the communication wonder and had the confidence and honesty to say, "Stacey, that's a good question, but I don't know the answer. I think you can name your company whatever you want, but I don't know the exact law on this. I suggest you call the New York City clerk's office to get the correct answer to your question." Stacey would have appreciated his truthful answer much more than the wrong information he spontaneously gave her. She would have obtained the correct information from the proper source and been able to give her company the right name from the start.

Admitting that you don't know something or that you are wrong is one of the easiest ways to instantly persuade people to trust and respect you. It lets people know that you have confidence in yourself and that you are open to hearing and learning new things. By admitting your fallibility you earn credibility so that when you stand before people and say, "Yes, I know the answer," they will believe you. The next time you are involved in a situation in which you are unsure of an answer to a question or you find out that you are wrong, say, "I don't know the answer" or "I'm wrong," loud and clear for anyone and everyone to hear. Use the situation as an opportunity to build a reputation as an honorable person with good character whose words can be trusted.

COMMUNICATION WONDER

Right Your Wrongs

Be sure to say to someone, "I don't know the
answer," or "I'm wrong," whenever you
are in a situation that warrants it.

Rule 7

· · · · ·

Don't
Take
Sides

IT COULD HAVE HAPPENED to anyone. You never imagined that what you said would backfire. Your friend was telling you about an argument she was having with her mother-in-law and you said, "I completely agree with you. Your mother-in-law is a very selfish woman. She's not a caring grandmother." Then, a few days later, you received distressing news. Your friend called to say, "My mother-in-law and I worked things out. We're not angry with each other anymore, but I'm very upset with you for what you said about her." You are totally puzzled by your friend's comment. All you did was agree with her and what she said about her mother-in-law. You were only trying to be supportive and now you have a problem. In the following stories you will see how friendly support can go too far, and you will learn what you can say to be a supportive friend without putting yourself in the line of fire.

My friend Jennifer innocently put herself in the line of fire when visiting her friend Lisa in Chicago. It happened one Friday night, just after Jennifer had arrived at Lisa's apartment. As she was unpacking her suitcase, she overheard Lisa on the phone with her younger sister, Robin. They were having a heated argument about Lisa's car. Lisa was refusing to lend Robin her car for the weekend.

When Lisa hung up she angrily told Jennifer, "My sister just called to tell me that she's coming to pick up my car, which is ridiculous because I never told her she could borrow it. She said I told her she could borrow it a month ago. Robin is being so manipulative and sneaky. I'll bet something exciting just came up for her to do, so she's pretending that I agreed to lend her my car. There's no way I agreed to that, because it was over a month ago that you and I made plans for this weekend. So I knew I would need my car. My sister is definitely lying. I can't stand it when she plays these mind games with me to get what she wants." Jennifer had met Robin only once and she didn't get a good feeling about her at the time. So in an effort to be supportive, Jennifer agreed with Lisa and criticized Robin. "It's terrible to have a sister who is such a liar. I don't know how you can trust her. Your sister should learn the values of honesty and integrity. When I met her she seemed really self-centered." "You're absolutely right," agreed Lisa. "I'm not lending her my car this weekend or ever again!" Jennifer and Lisa continued to talk about Robin for a bit longer, with Jennifer nodding in agreement with other negative statements Lisa made about her sister's behavior. Eventually their conversation shifted and they began to talk about all the things Lisa had planned for the weekend.

The time passed quickly and before Jennifer knew it, it was Sunday night and she was on a plane back to New York. She called Lisa a few days later to thank her again for the wonderful weekend. Then Jennifer asked Lisa if she had spoken to her sister since their fight on Friday. "Yes, I did," answered Lisa. "We worked everything out. Robin apologized and we're okay now. But, Jennifer, I need to talk to you about that." Jennifer had no idea what Lisa was about to say. "Do you remember how you told me that my sister was a liar and that she didn't have integrity? Well, that really bothered me. My sister and I are a lot alike and we were both brought up to know right from wrong. It's not like Robin did anything so terrible, she only asked to borrow my car. You had a lot of nerve saying those mean things about her."

Jennifer was shocked that Lisa was suddenly defending her sister. Jennifer recalled saying some things about Robin that weren't so nice, but for the most part she only repeated what Lisa had said about her own sister. Yet now that Lisa and Robin had patched things up, Jennifer was the one in trouble. Jennifer was amazed at how things had turned around and she wished she had been smart enough to keep her mouth shut from the beginning. She valued her friendship with Lisa and didn't want to start an argument. So instead of defending her position, Jennifer apologized. "I'm sorry for insulting your sister. I shouldn't have said what I said. I was just trying to be a good friend." But even after her apology, Lisa's only audible response was "uh-huh," and Jennifer was left with the feeling that all was not well between them.

This conversation alerted Jennifer to the fact that she had made a communication blunder when she took Lisa's side in the argument and harshly judged Robin. As an insider, Lisa was free to criticize her own sister, but as an outsider in this situation, Jennifer was not free to be critical of Lisa's sister. Lisa viewed her own criticism of her sister as situational and temporary, but she viewed Jennifer's criticism as an attack on her sister's character. Jennifer knew that in the future she would have to find a way to be supportive without being judgmental.

COMMUNICATION BLUNDER

It is a blunder to support someone in an argument by being critical of the person with whom she is arguing.

If it is a blunder to be on the side of your friend when she is in conflict with another person, then what do you do? In the next story you will learn what to say to maintain your neutrality and still be supportive. My friend Beth recently told me about an experience she had had some years ago during her junior year of college in Providence, Rhode Island. It left such an impression on her at the time that she still remembers most of the details today.

Beth, Wendy, Megan and Lily were friends in college who lived in the same dormitory and often socialized together on weekends. Wendy had a serious boyfriend named Jeff, who frequently hung out with them. Wendy and Jeff had been dating for over a year until one Saturday night when they had a huge blowup. Wendy told her girlfriends about the fight the following day. "I'm so angry. You won't believe it. Jeff and I broke up last night." All of Wendy's friends were surprised but happy to hear the news because none of them liked Jeff.

"What happened?" Megan asked inquisitively. Wendy explained, "Well, it all started at dinner last night when Jeff told me that he wants me to stay in Providence with him this summer because of the job he accepted. Right away I couldn't believe that he accepted a job in Providence without talking to me first because he knew that I had already accepted a summer job in New York with a top publishing house. I was so angry with him for expecting me to renege on my job commitment. And then, to top it off, he also told me that he turned down a job offer in New York. Can you believe that he could be so self-centered to do all that without mentioning one word about it to me? It's obvious that he cares more about his job than he does about me. I got so angry with him for what he did that I told him I never wanted to see him again. Then I got up and left him sitting in the restaurant."

Beth sat there quietly as Megan quickly jumped in to take Wendy's side. "Wow. I can't believe Jeff would expect you to break your commitment in New York just to please him. This proves what I've always thought. Jeff is a very selfish guy. You did the right thing by breaking up with him. If you ever married him, he would make you miserable. I always thought you were too good for him." "That's right," agreed Lily. "You did the right thing. You definitely shouldn't change your summer plans for him. I agree with you. Jeff is a self-centered, controlling guy. I'm so glad you found that out now. He's never going to change, and you deserve better."

Beth told me that at the time she didn't like Jeff either, but she recognized that he had some redeeming qualities that had kept Wendy interested in him for more than a year. Beth also knew from experience that arguments can be temporary and that many couples break up and then get back together. So she decided to handle the situation with the assumption that Wendy and Jeff would get back together. After Megan and Lily had finished their critical analysis of Jeff, Beth made some neutral yet supportive comments to encourage Wendy to do the talking. Beth said, "Wendy, it sounds like this is hard for you." "It is," Wendy responded. "I didn't sleep at all last night." Then Wendy went on to tell her friends more about the problem and how upset she was with Jeff. She added, "I really care about him. I thought we had a special relationship." Beth commented, "You seem really disappointed," and Wendy proceeded to talk about Jeff's good qualities and the good things in their relationship. Beth listened patiently, nodding to Megan and Lily every once in a while to encourage them to remain quiet so that Wendy would continue to share her feelings. When Wendy paused, Beth used it as an opportunity to make another supportive comment. "Wendy, it seems to me you have a lot to think about." "You're right, Beth, I do, but it's my problem and I have to figure out what I'm going to do. Thanks for listening." Before long Wendy seemed to calm down and the conversation about Jeff ended.

Within two days, just as Beth had suspected, Wendy and Jeff resolved their disagreement and were back together. Wendy told Beth that she and Jeff had agreed to live in different cities for the summer and that they would take turns visiting each other on weekends. Jeff apologized to her for making the job decision without talking to her and agreed that in the future he would not make any important decisions without talking to her first. Then Wendy apologized to Jeff for storming out of the restaurant. Wendy told Beth, "Please don't share these details with Megan and Lily. This time I don't want their opinions. I'm sure they won't be happy that we're back together again since they think so little of Jeff."

Beth wasn't surprised by this turn of events but she hoped that within a few days everything would return to normal. Unfortunately, the next week, Wendy said to Beth, "Jeff and I are going to his friend's party this weekend and he suggested that I invite my friends. Of course you're invited, but I'm not inviting Megan and Lily. Now that I know how much they dislike Jeff, I'm not comfortable being with him in their presence."

Beth felt bad that Wendy's relationships with Megan and Lily had suffered because of that one conversation about Jeff. But Beth was pleased with herself for saying the right thing at the right time to Wendy. What did she say? She used a communication wonder when she made nonjudgmental comments to Wendy to encourage her to talk about her problem with Jeff. Beth said, "It sounds like this is hard for you," "You seem really disappointed," and "It seems to me you have a lot to think about." By making these nonjudgmental comments Beth showed Wendy that she is a loyal, supportive friend.

What can we learn from Beth's experience? It is always best to assume that an argument between two people will be resolved and forgotten, while any judgments you make about other people involved in that argument will be remembered—forever.

•   •   •   •   •

COMMUNICATION WONDER

Don't Take Sides

Stay neutral when a friend is having an argument
with someone else. Make supportive comments
such as, "It sounds like this is hard for you,"
"You seem really disappointed" and "You
have a lot to think about" to encourage
your friend to talk while you listen.

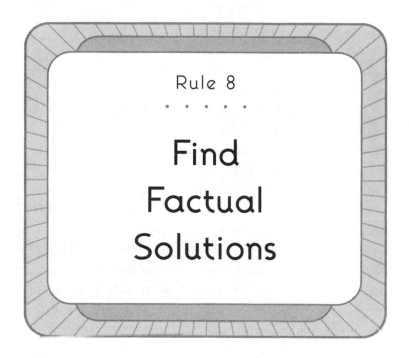

Rule 8

· · · · · ·

Find
Factual
Solutions

DISAGREEMENT IS NORMAL. It's a predictable part of life because each of us is unique, with different experiences, opinions and preferences. However, there are times when we are all alike. For example, almost all of us waste energy arguing about things that can easily be resolved. Have you ever gotten into a heated disagreement with a friend over the exact location or name of a restaurant? You thought the restaurant was uptown, she thought it was downtown; you said the name was Jack's and she said it was John's. Maybe you've gotten into an argument with a colleague when there was a disagreement about the date a project was due. You thought that your memory was better so you stuck to your position and tried to convince the other person to agree with you.

It's at times like these that you waste your energy because you think you are arguing about an opinion, but in reality you are arguing about a fact. Arguments about facts are foolish because there is always a specific, ascertainable solution. It is important to identify a factual disagreement so you can learn to say the right words at the right time to instantly persuade your friend to cooperate with you to end the conflict.

One day Kim got herself stuck in an unnecessary argument because she didn't realize that she was arguing about a fact, not an opinion. Kim and two college friends, Sarah and Theresa, decided to go on vacation together during the spring break of their senior year. They attended college in Boston, Massachusetts, where it was cold all winter, so they agreed to vacation somewhere in the Caribbean where they could expect warm weather, beautiful beaches and lots of sunbathing. Each of the girls lived on a budget so they were equally concerned about the cost of the trip. One evening while they were having dinner in their dormitory dining hall, the girls began discussing the details of their vacation, which was just three months away.

From the start, Sarah preferred to go to Puerto Rico while Kim and Theresa wanted to go to the Bahamas. Sarah began the conversation by calmly stating, "I think Puerto Rico is a better choice for us because it rains a lot in the Bahamas and I don't see any reason for us to take the chance of replacing our cold days in Boston with rainy days in the Bahamas." Kim said, "I think you're right, it probably does rain more in the Bahamas, but I still think going to the Bahamas is a better choice because of the exciting nightlife there. Everyone knows that tons of college students invade the Bahamas for spring break, so it has a great social scene." "That's a good point," agreed Sarah. Now Kim, thinking Sarah was beginning to feel more positive about going to the Bahamas, confidently added, "You know, Puerto Rico isn't an option for us anyway. It's not within our budget. A vacation in Puerto Rico would definitely be more expensive than a vacation in the Bahamas."

"What are you talking about?" Sarah responded curtly. She continued, "That's not true. A vacation in Puerto Rico in the spring, which is not high season, isn't any more expensive than a vacation in the Bahamas in the spring." "Yes it is. You're wrong," Kim answered. "It's obvious that the airfare from Boston to Puerto Rico is more expensive than the airfare from Boston to the Bahamas because Puerto Rico is farther away. And the hotels are more expensive in Puerto Rico as well." Sarah didn't like being told that she was wrong. "Kim," she said defensively, "both places are islands in the Caribbean, so I'm sure the hotels and airfares between Boston and both places are pretty much the same. You're just saying there's a price difference to persuade me to agree with you so that we all end up going to the Bahamas." Sarah's aggressive response angered Kim and made her stick to her position even more firmly. "Sarah, why do you think so many college kids choose to go to the Bahamas on vacation instead of Puerto Rico? It's because it's cheaper. Besides, there is no way I'm going to Puerto Rico. If you knew how expensive the trip to Puerto Rico would be, you wouldn't want to go there either." Sarah didn't appreciate Kim's insistence that she was right, nor did she like being told where she should spend her spring break. So she emphatically said, "I'm not going to the Bahamas! If you want to go there, then you two can go without me." Sarah got up and walked briskly out of the dining room.

Kim instantly regretted the way the discussion had turned

out. She looked at Theresa, who had kept quiet during the argument, and said, "I suppose I shouldn't have argued so hard about going to the Bahamas. But don't you agree that Puerto Rico is too expensive for us?" "I don't know," said Theresa. "But what I do know is that the two of you foolishly argued about the cost of the trip when all you had to do was agree to call the airlines and hotels directly to find out the actual prices. In minutes you would have had the correct answer and a solution to your problem."

Kim immediately knew that Theresa was right. Both Kim and Sarah got caught up defending their opinions about which vacation spot was cheaper, when in reality they were not arguing about opinions, they were arguing about objective facts that could easily have been proven true or false. Kim and Sarah each made a communication blunder when they allowed their discussion to turn into a contest of wills over who was right and who was wrong. If either Kim or Sarah had realized that they were engaged in a factual disagreement, one of them could have suggested that they find out the facts to quickly settle the dispute.

COMMUNICATION BLUNDER

It is a blunder to argue about something when there are facts available to resolve the disagreement.

In the next situation, you will meet some more people who chose to waste their time and energy arguing about something that could easily have been resolved. Jane and Robert, a married couple, were at home one Tuesday evening in March. When they had finished eating dinner and cleaning up the kitchen they went into the den to relax and watch their favorite television sitcom. The plot centered around the family's celebration of the grandfather's eighty-fifth birthday. The TV family was celebrating at a restaurant, and just as the waiter brought out the birthday cake and everyone started to sing "Happy Birthday," Jane sat up in her chair. "Robert!" she shouted. "We forgot that it's your mother's birthday next week, on April seventh. I can't believe we would have completely forgotten about it if it wasn't for this show. You know, we already have dinner plans with your parents for this Saturday night. Why don't we celebrate her birthday then? I'll call the restaurant to order a cake and ask them to put some candles on it and we can surprise her with it at dessert, okay?"

"What?" Robert asked, "I didn't forget about her birthday. It's not next week, it's at the end of the month, on the twenty-seventh. Don't you remember that we all celebrated it together last year at the end of April after we returned from our trip to Canada?" "Robert, of course I remember our trip last year, but I also remember that it wasn't at the end of April. Your timing is off. I distinctly remember buying your mother a present right after we returned from Canada, and that was at the beginning of April," said Jane, who felt completely satisfied that she had proven her point.

That is, until Robert chimed in, "Nope, you're wrong. It's you who has the dates mixed up. Don't you think I know the date of my mother's birthday?" Jane was sure Robert was mistaken. He was always more forgetful than her and she wished that he wouldn't become so defensive every time he forgot something and she pointed it out to him.

"Robert," she stated, "we didn't go to Canada at the end of April, we went at the beginning of April and I'll prove it to you." Jane got up and went into the bedroom to get her photo album. She knew she had written the dates of the trip on the back of each picture and she would show Robert the pictures to prove her point.

When Jane found her evidence she marched back into the den and showed Robert the pictures. "See," she said, pointing at the back of the pictures. "Look at the dates. They say 'Toronto, Canada, April 2–6.' So there. I'm right." Robert looked at the pictures but still wasn't convinced. "Jane, I see the pictures. So I agree with you now that we went to Canada at the beginning of April, but I still disagree with you about the date of my mother's birthday. We didn't celebrate her birthday right after we returned home. We celebrated it later that month." Jane couldn't stand this circular conversation that continued because of Robert's pointless stubbornness. "Okay, enough," she said, throwing her hands up. "I give up. I know you're wrong. You can ignore your mother's birthday and insult her, but I'm not going to do that. I'm going to call the restaurant to order a birthday cake for her and I'm also going to get her a present with a card that says 'from Jane.'" "You're being totally ridiculous!" responded Robert. "Why don't you just forget about the whole thing for now and watch TV? It's my mother we're talking about, not yours."

Jane could not calmly return to watching TV. She was annoyed with Robert for being stubborn and for relentlessly disagreeing with her, especially when she was right. Jane couldn't wait for Saturday to arrive so she could prove to Robert that he was wrong.

What happened here? Jane and Robert each made a communication blunder when they argued over a fact—the date of Robert's mother's birthday. They let their egos get the best of them and wasted their energy trying to prove who was right and who had the better memory. By trying to win an argument that could easily have been resolved by obtaining a single piece of information, Robert and Jane created unnecessary friction in their marriage.

What should have happened? One of them should have realized they were disagreeing about a fact—Robert's mother's birth date. Then, that person should have said, "Wait a minute, we're arguing over a fact and there's no point in doing that. So let's stop arguing and find out the information that will resolve this disagreement." Instead of arguing about the fact, Robert and Jane should have cooperated with each other to find the quick and easy factual solution to their problem. In this case that would not only have stopped the argument, it would also have prevented them from offending Robert's mother by getting the date of her birthday wrong. Robert could have said, "Let's call my sister right now and ask her the date." Or Jane could have said, "I'll call your father at work tomorrow to ask him for the date." By getting that one little piece of information, Jane and Robert would have ended their confrontation and been able to spend an enjoyable evening together watching television.

Engaging in an argument over a fact is a waste of everyone's time and energy. It creates conflict that could easily be avoided. Use this communication wonder to help you discover what is causing your argument. Is it an unknown fact or a difference of opinion? If you conclude that you are arguing about a fact, make a cooperative effort with your friend, family member or colleague to stop arguing and find out the fact that would accurately determine who is right and who is wrong. This is the path toward better communication and peaceful relationships. Bear in mind, it takes two people to start an argument, but only one to stop it.

COMMUNICATION WONDER

Find Factual Solutions

When you are in a disagreement, ask yourself, "Are we arguing about facts or opinions?" If you conclude that you are arguing over facts, stop arguing and get the facts to resolve the issue.

Rule 9

· · · · ·

Hold Your Tongue

YOU ARE ENJOYING LUNCH with your friend when she tells you she is very upset. She has a major problem and doesn't know what to do about it. She tells you her problem and you think she's making a mountain out of a molehill because you have a simple solution. You tell her what you think she should do to resolve it, but shockingly, she gets angry with you and says harshly, "It's really none of your business." Apparently, you put your foot in your mouth. You can't understand why she told you about her problem if she didn't want your advice.

How many times have you been in a situation like this? More than likely, you thought you were only doing what any good friend would do. After all, why would someone tell you a problem if not to hear what you have to say about it? Well, sometimes caring words of advice can touch a nerve and set off an unpredictable reaction. Although friends can help each other by offering a new perspective on a problem, that perspective is not always wanted. How do you know when your advice is wanted? In the following stories, you will see how good intentions can lead to a communication blunder that strains a relationship, and you will learn a communication wonder for figuring out when you should and should not give advice.

One day Jon comes home from work and his wife, Erica, is on the phone talking to her mother. She seems annoyed with her mother again as she turns to Jon and shakes her head with her familiar "Here she goes again, telling me what to do" expression on her face. When she hangs up Jon asks her what happened. "Oh, she was criticizing my new hairstyle. She said she doesn't like it; it's too short and unflattering. I hate it when she criticizes me."

Jon can't understand why his wife doesn't tell her mother to keep her critical comments to herself. He innocently says, "Erica, you should stand up to your mother. You should have told her that it's your hair, on your head, and you like your new hairstyle. Maybe she keeps criticizing you because you never answer her back. Don't you notice that she doesn't criticize your sister because she speaks up?" "That's not true," his wife says loudly. "How would you know what my mother says to my sister?" "Well, I've been around them enough to know that your mother is much more critical of you. How can you not see that?" Erica didn't ask for her husband's advice and she doesn't like being told what to do, so she says, "You don't know what you're talking about. Besides, you have no right to tell me how to handle my mother. I don't tell you what to say to your mother, and believe me, she's no gem." "What's my mother got to do with this?" Jon demands to know. "Everything," yells his wife. "If you're going to tell me how to handle my mother, then I'm going to tell you how to handle your mother!" Jon realizes that the conversation is getting out of control and he doesn't undertand what happened. It was only minutes before that Erica was annoyed with her mother; now she's angry at him and insulting his mother. He can't understand why Erica became so defensive. He was just trying to help. What did he do wrong?

Jon made a communication blunder when he gave Erica unsolicited advice. He didn't realize that his wife had not asked him a question like, "What do you think about the situation?" or "Do you have an opinion about how I should handle my mother?" So when he gave her unsolicited advice she wasn't prepared to listen to it; rather, she was set to defend herself against it. Giving someone unsolicited advice often turns a peaceful conversation into an argument. In this next story, involving Jane and Pat, you will observe another example of how well-intentioned advice can create conflict between friends.

Jane and Pat are at a restaurant having Sunday brunch. Jane asked Pat to invite Roger, her new boyfriend, to join them. She thought that this would be a nice way for her to meet him. But Pat came alone to the restaurant. Jane is disappointed and casually asks Pat why Roger couldn't join them. "He's hardly ever available on weekends," she says. This surprises Jane, so she asks her why he is so busy on the weekends. "His mother is old and not well, so he spends most of his weekends with her," she replies. "That's strange," Jane says. "Have you ever had plans with him on the weekend?" "No," Pat says. "I've told him I want to go with him to visit his mother, but he says I would be bored because all they do is stay in the house and watch TV. Actually, just between us, I do feel a little left out, but I expect he'll ask me to go with him soon."

Now Jane is suspicious of Roger's behavior because she's never met a single man who spends his weekends with his aging mother. She is concerned because she knows that Pat really likes him. She says, "You know what, Pat? Maybe he's married. You should find a way to check up on him." Pat is completely stunned. "He is not married!" she says. "What do you take me for, an idiot? You don't know how nice he is. You've never met him so you don't know what you're talking about." Jane is shocked by Pat's defensiveness. She didn't say anything bad about Pat, she simply wanted to make her friend aware of her boyfriend's unusual behavior. Now she wishes she hadn't said anything at all. "All right, Pat. I'm probably wrong. Just forget what I said." They changed the subject and continued their meal, but Pat seemed cold and distant the whole time.

Jane had Pat's best interests in mind when she gave her unsolicited advice. But Pat didn't ask for Jane's advice and wasn't prepared to hear it. She perceived Jane's words as criticism and automatically defended herself. When someone does not want your advice, beware! Almost any suggestion or solution you give that person at that time will be a communication blunder.

COMMUNICATION BLUNDER

Giving someone unsolicited advice
is a communication blunder.

Does this mean you should never give advice unless specifically asked for it? No, not necessarily. There is a way to encourage someone to give you permission to share your advice. In the story below, about Jake and Dan, we explore the communication blunder in more detail and you will learn the communication wonder you should use to share your advice without creating conflict.

Jake and Dan are sitting together at a coffee shop when Dan tells Jake that he is very upset about his job situation. He dislikes his current job and has been looking for a new one for a few months, but without success. Dan is discouraged because he has had a few interviews but never made it past the first interview. He tells Jake that he knows his experience makes him a qualified job applicant, so he can't understand why he hasn't gotten any job offers. Jake assumes there must be some reason why Dan isn't faring well. To be helpful, he tries to figure out what Dan is saying or doing in his interviews that might be turning the interviewers off. "Dan, when the interviewers ask you why you want to leave your current job, what do you say?" "I usually say that I like the work I do, but I feel stifled because I need to rely on my colleagues to get things done and they are simply incompetent. They're just not as creative or hardworking as I am. In fact, I've come up with a lot of good ideas, but they never want to work with me to implement them. The people I work with make it hard for me to accomplish anything." As Jake listens to Dan's answer he thinks he might have figured out the problem. So he says, "Dan, I think your answer leaves too much room for misinterpretation. Your interviewers don't know your colleagues and they don't know you, either. How are they supposed to know who has the problem? They might think no one wants to implement your ideas because they're bad or because no one wants to work with you. Your comments could make it look like you're the one who's incompetent. You better watch what you say."

"What?" Dan exclaims. "Since when are you the expert on how to interview? You don't have any idea what you're talking about. In fact, I think my interviewers appreciate my honesty. The only time I say something negative is when I talk about my colleagues. If I only said positive things about my current job then there would obviously be no reason for me to be looking for a new one. What you're saying makes absolutely no sense!" Jake is stunned by Dan's anger. In an effort to calm things down, he says, "You told me your problem so I was just giving you my advice." "Thanks, but no thanks. I don't need you to tell me what to do." Dan gets up. On his way out he says, "I'll catch you later." Jake is left wondering what happened. He didn't mean to anger his friend, but somehow he did.

Jake made a communication blunder because he assumed that Dan wanted his advice even though he didn't ask for it. Dan may have shared his job concerns with Jake, but that didn't mean he wanted Jake to tell him what to do.

What should Jake have done? First, Jake should have been aware that Dan did not ask for his advice. Second, because Dan didn't ask for advice, he shouldn't have forced it on him. Third, since Jake wanted to give Dan some helpful advice, he should have set the situation up to motivate Dan to ask for it. Jake could easily have done this by using the communication wonder to seek permission to speak his mind. Jake should have asked, "Would you like my advice?" before blurting out his suggestions. This communication wonder is a simple way to show respect for someone. If Dan had said no, he didn't want Jake's advice, then Jake would have known to hold his tongue no matter what. If Dan had said yes, he wanted Jake's advice, then Jake would have had permission to tell Dan what he thought about the situation. Once Dan chose to listen to Jake's suggestions, he would have been prepared to listen without becoming defensive and argumentative.

This communication wonder works because it shows respect and shows the other person that you are trying to be helpful rather than critical. When your intentions are good and you want to be helpful, start by asking for permission to share your advice. Remember, the decision about whether you should share your advice with a friend, family member or colleague always rests in their hands, not yours.

COMMUNICATION WONDER

Hold Your Tongue

Give advice only when:
(1) you are asked for it; or
(2) you get permission to give it after asking, "Would you like my advice?"

Rule 10

· · · · ·

Beware of Uncomplimentary Compliments

IS A COMPLIMENT ALWAYS what it seems? Have you ever received a compliment that you didn't really want? Has anyone ever said something to you like "I really like your new hairstyle. It makes your face look thinner"? Your first response might be to say, "Thank you," but as you walk away you might suddenly realize that she just insulted you by telling you that you have a fat face. Did she mean to insult you? Probably not, but the comment was hurtful and insulting anyway. Your friend gave you an uncomplimentary compliment. Most often, uncomplimentary compliments are unintentional because people think that their words are thoughtful and kind when in reality they are not.

How can you be sure that the compliments you give are always desired and welcomed so that you don't offend someone you meant to praise? These stories will show you how to identify an uncomplimentary compliment. Then you will learn the rule for a quick and easy way to prevent yourself from ever making an uncomplimentary compliment again.

Sam and Jack are good friends. Sam was laid off from his job as director of marketing at a shoe company about two months ago. Since then he's applied for a number of marketing positions at other companies. During a telephone conversation, Sam tells Jack that he's excited about an interview that he has the next day. It's for a position as director of marketing at a shoe company that rivals his old employer. Sam thinks he has a good shot at getting the job. "That's great," Jack says. Jack hopes Sam gets the job, because he knows Sam's been very anxious since he's been out of work and his bills have been accumulating. Jack remembers that the last time Sam was looking for a job, more than five years ago, he had trouble getting past the first round of interviews. At the time, Jack thought it was because of Sam's noticeably passive attitude. However, since Sam got married three years ago, Jack has noticed that he has become a lot more confident and assertive.

Since Jack wants to boost Sam's confidence for his interview he says, "Sam, I'm sure the interview will go well. You have a lot of knowledge about the shoe industry and since the last time you were job hunting, you've become much more assertive and secure with yourself. I know that will come across in your interview." Sam gives Jack a hesitant "Thank you," but is upset because he didn't know that anyone, especially Jack, thought that he used to be passive and insecure. Sam doesn't feel like talking about the job interview anymore so he tells Jack that he has to go because he has things to do. Jack is surprised by Sam's abrupt ending of the conversation, but figures he is busy. Jack wishes him good luck for his interview and hangs up the phone.

Jack doesn't know that he gave Sam an uncomplimentary compliment. Jack complimented Sam on his business knowledge but then counteracted that compliment by telling him that he is more secure and assertive now than he was the last time he was looking for a job. If Jack had thought about the implications of what he said, that Sam used to be insecure and passive, he might have realized that his compliment was not a compliment but an insult. Any comment that compares now with an earlier time is a communication blunder because it automatically suggests that something was previously negative.

One day Cindy was slowly walking through one of the aisles at a Barnes and Noble bookstore in search of a book that one of her friends had recommended. As she looked up, she saw the profile of an attractive, well-dressed woman who looked familiar. After a moment Cindy realized that the woman, Elizabeth, was the mother of one of the children in her son's kindergarten class. Cindy remembered that the last time she had seen Elizabeth she was dropping her son off at school and wearing a T-shirt, sweatpants and no makeup. In the bookstore Cindy smiled at her and Elizabeth smiled back with a look of recognition on her face. As they moved closer to each other Cindy noticed how attractive Elizabeth looked fully made up and stylishly dressed. "Hi, how are you doing?" Cindy asked. "I'm doing well," Elizabeth replied, "and how about you?" Cindy answered, "Fine," and then went on to say,

"You look terrific today, Elizabeth. I barely recognize you with makeup." "Thanks," Elizabeth replied with a questioning tone in her voice and a strange, bewildered look on her face. "Well, I have to run now," she said. "I suppose we'll be seeing each other at school before long." "Yes, I guess so," Cindy said, as Elizabeth turned away. Cindy instantly thought that maybe she had said or done something wrong because of the strange look on Elizabeth's face after she complimented her, but she couldn't imagine what. All she did was say how terrific Elizabeth looked. Cindy assumed that Elizabeth was probably having a bad day and that the next time they saw each other things would be different.

In this story Cindy made a communication blunder because she followed up a positive comment with a comment that implied that Elizabeth looked terrific only because she was wearing makeup and that when she had seen her without makeup Elizabeth looked lousy. Comparing the way she looks now to the way she looked before is a "before and after" comparison compliment and is always uncomplimentary.

COMMUNICATION BLUNDER

It is a blunder to give a before-and-after comparison compliment.

This last story is another example of the wrong thing to say. Then you will learn the communication wonder that prevents you from accidentally insulting someone you intended to praise.

Janice and Marion are sisters-in-law who haven't seen each other in six months. On this day, they and their husbands have been invited to their mother-in-law's home for dinner. As the dinner hour gets closer Marion is still unsure about what to wear. She wants to look stylish but not too dressed up. Since the last time she saw her sister- and brother-in-law she's lost more than ten pounds so she's intent on wearing just the right outfit to show off her figure.

At 6:20 P.M. Marion is ready to go. She has decided to wear a new pair of black slacks, a sleeveless knit top and heels. She is feeling good about how she looks and is eager to go. About ten minutes after she and her husband arrive at her mother-in-law's house, the doorbell rings. Marion and her mother-in-law walk to the front door to greet Janice and her husband. After the greetings, Marion's mother-in-law suggests that they all go into the den to have drinks and hors d'oeuvres. They head to the den and Marion and Janice sit down next to each other. Janice tells Marion, "You look great." Marion responds, "Thanks. I lost weight. I've been dieting for a while." Janice answers, "You know, I can tell. Your behind looks smaller." Marion can't believe her ears. She thinks to herself, "What was that supposed to be? A compliment or an insult? Am I supposed to say thank you?"

After Janice's comment, Marion feels uncomfortable and excuses herself to go to the bathroom. She looks at herself in the mirror and carefully checks out her body from both a front and a rear view. After calming down and realizing that Janice probably didn't mean anything bad by the compliment, Marion returns to the den but sits down next to her husband. Marion can't help but feel self-conscious and insulted by Janice's remark. Concerned about what else Janice might say to her, Marion decides to keep some distance between them. Janice notices that Marion did not sit next to her, but doesn't think much about it. She assumes they'll catch up on family matters later that evening.

What happened here? Janice made a communication blunder when she told Marion that she looks great and followed this with a comment about how her behind looks smaller. A comment is a compliment only when it tells someone something completely positive about him- or herself. Because of Janice's comment, Marion felt uncomfortable around Janice and kept her distance.

How could Janice have avoided making this communication blunder? The answer is simple: Before Janice opened her mouth to give the compliment, she should have asked herself, "Am I about to give a before-and-after comparison compliment?" Janice would have realized that telling Marion that her behind looks smaller *now* than it did *before* she lost weight is a communication blunder because it implies that Janice used to think that Marion was unattractive. Instead, Janice should·have said, "Marion, you look great," and stopped there, without any mention of how Marion's weight loss had affected her behind.

Now that you know all about uncomplimentary compliments, be alert so that you don't unknowingly give one to someone. Before you open your mouth to pay a compliment, ask yourself whether it includes a before-and-after comparison. If it does, then it's best to cut the compliment in half and share only the positive part that relates to how the person is now, without any mention of what he or she was like before.

COMMUNICATION WONDER

Beware of Uncomplimentary Compliments

Before you give someone a compliment, ask yourself, "Is this a before-and-after comparison?" If the answer is yes, then cut the compliment in half and share only the after part.

Rule 11

· · · · ·

Magnify Praise

EVERY PERSON IS UNIQUE. Each of us has a different favorite food, a different favorite movie, a different ideal job and different personal goals. But there is one way that every one of us, regardless of race, religion, nationality or gender, is exactly alike. Every one of us has the same basic human need to be appreciated. When you recognize someone for doing something well and you tell that person about it, you make him feel especially good. When your words make someone feel appreciated and valued, you instantly persuade that person to appreciate and value you. It's the revolving-door principle: what goes around comes around. In the following stories you will discover how to say the right thing, at the right time, to the right person to magnify your praise and put a smile on everyone's face.

Mr. Stillman is a partner at a law firm and he is overseeing the work of three associates on a particular legal case. The associates, Dawn, Jack and Stephanie, are due in his office in a half hour for a team meeting. Each of the three associates was assigned a different task in relation to the case. Dawn's assignment was to write the first draft of a legal brief in support of a motion to dismiss the case against their client. She finished the draft the day before and has already turned it in to Mr. Stillman. In the brief, Dawn laid out the arguments for why the claims against their client should be dismissed, and she offered examples of prior cases with outcomes supporting those arguments. The final brief will be submitted to the judge the following week to help him make his decision on the issue. Mr. Stillman is hoping that the brief will persuade the judge to rule in favor of their client and dismiss the case so that it doesn't go to trial.

About a half hour before the team meeting, Mr. Stillman finally finds the time to review Dawn's brief. He thought he might have to delay the meeting to give himself more time to edit it, but, as he sits at his desk reading the brief, he realizes that a half hour is more than enough time to review it. He thinks to himself, "She needs to make a few changes, but overall, it's an exceptionally good first draft. Dawn must have spent a lot of time working on this project because her research and writing is persuasive and on point. I wish every associate would work this hard and do such a good job."

Mr. Stillman finishes reviewing the brief just as Dawn, Jack and Stephanie enter his office to begin the team meeting. Mr. Stillman first mentions that the final version of Dawn's brief is due next week. He considers praising Dawn in front of the other two associates for the hard work and time she put into researching her arguments and the high quality of her writing. But after a moment's thought he decides to keep his compliments to himself. His concern is that praising Dawn in front of the others might embarrass her. Or, if he praises her, but doesn't praise Jack and Stephanie at the same time, he might insult them. So Mr. Stillman chooses not to say anything about Dawn and moves on to the next topic. He asks Jack and Stephanie to report on the status of their work as it relates to the case. After listening to their responses, Mr. Stillman feels comfortable with the status of everyone's work and ends the meeting. He says, "Dawn, please stay here. I have something to discuss with you. Jack and Stephanie, I'll see you later today."

Jack and Stephanie exit the office, leaving Mr. Stillman and Dawn sitting in their chairs looking at each other. Dawn knows how hard she worked on the brief and she believes she did a really good job, but now she is worried as she sits there waiting for Mr. Stillman to begin talking. Mr. Stillman quickly skims Dawn's brief and looks up. "Dawn, this is extremely well written. I can tell that you put a lot of time into this brief. You did a great job on it. You should be proud of yourself. Now let's go over some small details that need to be changed." Dawn instantly feels relieved and says, "Thank you for saying that, Mr. Stillman. It means a lot to me coming from you. I appreciate it." Mr. Stillman and Dawn review the brief, and at the end of their discussion, he asks, "Dawn, I know it's Thursday, but do you think you will be able to prepare a revised version of this document by five P.M. tomorrow so I can do a final reading over the weekend?" "Sure," Dawn replies enthusiastically. She knows she can complete the minor changes by then and, surprisingly, is eager to work late again on the revisions even though the brief has already demanded so much of her time. Dawn walks out of the office happy that Mr. Stillman is so pleased with her work.

It seems like everything went just fine, right? Mr. Stillman gave Dawn a compliment. He treated her with respect and appreciation. So what's the problem? The problem is that he didn't recognize and seize the wonderful opportunity that was staring him in the face. Mr. Stillman had the chance to praise Dawn in front of the other two associates for her excellent work, but he didn't. He thought the praise was best said in private. He didn't want to embarrass Dawn or insult Jack and Stephanie. Mr. Stillman didn't realize that giving praise in public for a job well done magnifies the power of the compliment and provides positive reinforcement and motivation for everyone who hears it.

If Mr. Stillman had praised Dawn in public, she might have felt a little uncomfortable because it's rare that someone praises another person in public. However, it makes a big impression. Dawn would have known that Mr. Stillman thought so highly of her work that he wanted other people to be aware of her skills. And since people believe what they hear from someone they respect, Mr. Stillman's public recognition of Dawn's exceptional work would have had a carryover effect by persuading Stephanie and Jack to respect Dawn for her work. In turn, Dawn would have been persuaded to appreciate her boss because of his willingness to present her in a such a positive light to others.

The public praise would also have served to motivate Dawn, Jack and Stephanie. Dawn would have felt doubly proud of herself and eager to work as hard on the next project to please her boss and live up to her newly acquired reputation as a skilled lawyer. Jack and Stephanie would have instantly known that Mr. Stillman recognizes and appreciates quality work. Since Jack and Stephanie didn't submit a brief at the same time as Dawn, they would not have been insulted by Mr. Stillman's singling her out for praise. Instead, they would have been motivated to work hard on their assignments, so that the next time they would be the recipients of his praise.

COMMUNICATION BLUNDER

It is a blunder to miss an opportunity
to praise someone in public for
something he or she did well.

Here is another example of how praising in public instantly energizes a relationship. During a telephone conversation with her mother, Ann, Michelle mentioned how excited she was about the upcoming seminar she was going to give at a university in Cambridge, Massachusetts. "Oh," Ann said, "that reminds me of something. Your father said the nicest thing about me last night." "Really? What was it?" Michelle asked. Eagerly her mother responded, "We were out to dinner with Ruth and Eddie Herman, and Ruth asked me how you were doing. I told her that you were almost finished writing the manuscript for your book. I also told her that next week you are flying up to Cambridge to present a seminar to students, staff and professors. Then Ruth said something about the fact that you are really dedicated to your work and I said, 'Yes, she is. I'm really proud of her and all her accomplishments. Michelle loves what she's doing and works very hard at it.'"

"Wait," Michelle said when her mother paused, "what does any of this have to do with the nice thing that Dad said about you?"

"Well, I'm getting to that. Apparently your father overheard my conversation with Ruth because he stopped talking to Eddie and said to Ruth, 'I'm proud of Michelle, too. But Ruth, I'm equally proud of Ann. I'm sure she didn't tell you about her role in all of this. I have to give her credit for being such a devoted mother to both of our daughters. Last weekend she set aside a day so that she could be home to listen to Michelle practice her presentation. My wife is really something special.' Wasn't that nice of your father to say that about me in front of Ruth and Eddie? I can't tell you how good that made me feel. I just sat there and smiled. I felt like leaning over to give him a kiss right then and there." "Mom, I can just imagine how you felt. You know you really do deserve the credit. I'm glad that Dad recognizes what an unusually caring and supportive mother you are." "But Michelle, it got even better. Right after your father gave me this compliment, Ruth turned to me and said, 'It's so nice that he thinks so much of you.' With all these compliments, I was in a great mood for the rest of the night."

Without knowing it, Ann's husband had used a communication wonder to make her feel good about herself and her relationship with him. By taking a moment to praise Ann in public he magnified the power and effect of a compliment that would have been nice but less memorable if he had said it to her in private. With public praise he sent her a strong message that he recognizes and appreciates all of her efforts. His praise told her that he thinks her actions are so extraordinary that other people should know about them. Ann instantly appreciated her husband for the words of praise he gave her in front of their friends.

It is easy to magnify praise. It is a matter of recognizing and using an opportunity when it presents itself. Use this communication wonder to appreciate and value others and you will persuade them to appreciate and value you.

COMMUNICATION WONDER

Magnify Praise

Seize the opportunity to sincerely praise someone in public whenever he or she has done something worthy.

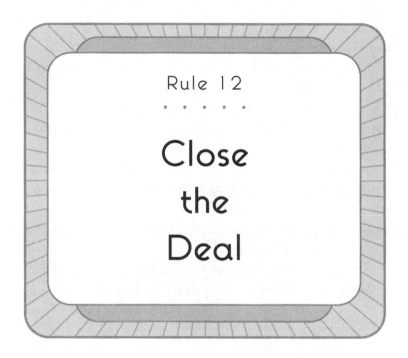

Rule 12

· · · · ·

Close
the
Deal

WHEN I MEDIATE A legal dispute I facilitate communication between the plaintiff and the defendant by asking questions and encouraging them to listen to each other explain what led to the dispute. If they are able to cooperate and come to a voluntary agreement, they can avoid having to plead their case before a judge. Everyone feels relieved and satisfied when an agreement is reached, but that doesn't end the mediation process. Once we've reached an agreement, it's time to hammer out the specifics of the settlement and close the deal. One of the worst mistakes I can make as a mediator is to write up a settlement agreement that leaves unanswered questions that could force clients back into mediation or into a courtroom to resolve those issues. For example, if a settlement provides that the defendant will pay the plaintiff a sum of money, some specific questions that need to be answered are: Will the money be paid as a lump sum or in installments? On what date or dates will it be paid and by what method— check, money order, by mail or by hand? If someone agrees to return a malfunctioning product, we must determine the answers to questions such as: When will the item be returned to the store? Who will receive the item? What should the person expect to receive—store credit or a cash refund? A successful settlement gets rid of assumptions, clarifies expectations and creates accountability.

Through my mediation experiences, I have discovered that differing expectations can frequently be the cause of unnecessary stress, wasted energy and conflicts in our personal and professional lives. After seeing the value of hammering out the specifics in mediations, I began to include this mediation technique in my everyday conversations and in the Instant Persuasion rules I designed and taught to others. The following stories illustrate that clarifying expectations by creating a concrete plan of action is what closes a deal and prevents future conflicts.

Hillary and Andrew are newly married. They both work full-time at demanding jobs. At this particular time in their relationship, Hillary is unhappy because Andrew isn't helping her with the household chores. She decides to raise the issue with him and is pleasantly surprised to find that he readily agrees to participate more with the chores. Unfortunately, over the next week, Hillary barely notices any change in the level of Andrew's participation in doing the chores around the house. Hillary becomes upset and angry with him, not only

because she continues to bear the burden of the domestic responsibilities, but also because she has discovered that she
cannot trust Andrew to follow through on the agreement he
made with her.

One evening after dinner Hillary's frustration comes to a
head. Hillary is loading the dishwasher after eating the dinner
that she prepared for Andrew and herself. She glances into
the living room and sees her husband comfortably relaxing on
the couch reading a magazine. It has been a difficult day for
Hillary at work. She is tired and irritable and the sight of him
sitting on the couch relaxing triggers her anger. "Andrew, can't
you get up and help me with the dishes? Last week you agreed
to help more around the house and since then I haven't seen
you do anything. Did you forget about our agreement or were
you just telling me what you thought I wanted to hear?" Andrew doesn't like that accusation. He gets up and walks into
the kitchen to respond. "I am helping out, just like I said I
would. I've been taking out the garbage every morning. Maybe
you haven't noticed because I leave for work after you." "That's
it? That's how you're helping?" exclaims Hillary. "I expected
you to take on a lot more of the chores. That means doing
some of things that I've been doing all along, like the laundry,
making the bed, emptying the dishwasher, going to the supermarket, making dinner. How can you possibly think that taking out the garbage is enough?" "Well, you didn't say it wasn't.
I thought you'd appreciate any help you got from me. I guess
it doesn't matter what I do. Nothing I do would be good
enough for you." "That's not true. You're just looking for an excuse to avoid doing more chores. Take a look around the house.
Don't you see all the things that need to be done?" "Calm
down, Hillary. You don't have to get so angry about this. If

you'd told me what you wanted me to do to help in the first place, I would have done it."

Andrew is right. Hillary made a communication blunder when she didn't clarify the specifics of what she meant when she asked him to "help more around the house." How could she hold Andrew accountable when she never stated her expectations? She was satisfied with his agreement to help and assumed that they both understood the meaning of the word "help." Unfortunately, Hillary didn't close the deal when she left the meaning of "help" open to individual interpretation. Inevitably, Hillary ended up disappointed with the outcome and angry with her husband.

COMMUNICATION BLUNDER

It is a blunder to neglect to work out the specific details of an agreement.

Clarifying the details of an agreement avoids conflicts and reduces the needless waste of time and energy. Jennifer's story teaches us a valuable lesson. One Saturday Jennifer received an unexpected bill in the mail from her doctor's medical group. It was for $50 for a medical test she had taken some months earlier. She called her doctor's office to find out why she had received the bill when she knew it should have been paid by her insurance company. Jennifer had to listen to the computerized voice response, press a series of numbers and then wait on hold for another five minutes until a woman picked up her call. She asked to speak to somebody in the billing department and once again was put on hold and had to wait until a second woman picked up and asked, "Hello, how can I help you?" Jennifer explained, "I just received a bill for a strep throat culture that I had two months ago. My insurance company should have covered the charge. I think your office needs to bill my insurance company, not me." The assistant understood the complaint and offered to look up Jennifer's record on her computer. She took Jennifer's full name, social security information and the name of the doctor she used in the office. After another minute she said, "Ah, I see the problem. The computer doesn't list that test as 'medically necessary,' so your insurance company won't cover it." "What? It was a test for strep throat. There would have been no reason for me to take that test unless I was sick! Doesn't that mean it is medically necessary?" "Okay," said the assistant, "there must be a mistake in our records. I'll talk to your doctor and get his approval to correct the error." Jennifer felt relieved because she thought everything was settled and the problem was resolved. "Thanks for your help," she said and hung up. Feeling satisfied with the outcome of the phone call, Jennifer threw the bill into the garbage.

A couple of weeks later, Jennifer opened her mail to find a duplicate bill from her doctor's medical group for the same medical test! Now she was annoyed because she knew she would have to deal with the problem all over again. She thought to herself, "This doctor and his staff don't know what they're doing." It was too late to call the doctor's office that day, so Jennifer waited until the next morning. When the clock struck 9 A.M., she reached for the phone. Again, she had to listen to the computerized voice response that seemed like a verbal maze. Eventually the computerized voice told her that someone would be with her shortly. As the minutes passed, Jennifer became more and more agitated with her doctor and the assistants for their inefficient service. Finally, someone took her call. "Hello, I need to speak with the woman who takes care of billing." Jennifer waited on hold another minute until she was connected to a man who asked, "How can I help you today?" She greeted him and said, "The last time I called about my bill I spoke to a woman. She knows my situation so I'd like to talk to her again. Is she there?" The assistant responded, "I don't know who you're referring to. There are three women and two men who work in this office. We manage everything for the ten doctors and their patients in this group. What was the woman's name?" "I don't know. She had a raspy voice," said Jennifer, who was annoyed with herself for not writing down the woman's name. "Never mind," she continued. "Why don't I just explain the problem to you so you can help me. By the way, what's your name?"

He told her his name was Jon Weaver, and then Jennifer explained her situation all over again. Jon looked up her record in the computer. "I see that the test you're talking about is still not coded as 'medically necessary' and you owe fifty dollars. Maybe the woman you spoke to hasn't spoken to your doctor yet. The doctors are so busy here. We rarely have time to talk to them about particular billing issues. Sometimes things like this take longer than expected. I'll look into it, okay?" No, this time it wasn't okay with Jennifer. She knew better. She wasn't going to make the same blunder she made the last time by ending the conversation without closing the deal. She wanted a specific plan of action to be sure that this payment problem would be cleared up. So she said, "Jon, thank you for looking into it. I'd like us to work out the specifics of where we're going from here. Are you saying that you will speak to my doctor and correct the mistake, or that you are going to pass my billing problem on to someone else?" "Well, I can talk to your doctor about this myself," Jon replied. "Great. Will you be able to speak to my doctor today?" "I'll try. But if I don't get to him today, I'll talk to him tomorrow." "Thank you. Would you please call me after you speak to him to let me know that this matter is cleared up? If I'm not in, please leave me a message." "Sure, no problem. What's your phone number?" Jennifer gave him her cell phone number and then just before they hung up she said, "Jon, can I please have your direct phone number? If for some reason I don't hear from you by four P.M. tomorrow, can I call you?" "Sure. Here's my number," responded Jon. Jennifer wrote down his name, phone number, the date and the 4 P.M. deadline on the back of the bill.

Jennifer hung up feeling satisfied because this time she had designed a way to follow up on Jon to be sure that he followed through on their agreement. She had his name and phone number so she could hold him accountable for whatever happened. She had him agree to personally take care of correcting the billing error himself. And, she knew where to reach him if he didn't reach her by 4 P.M. the next day. This deadline would motivate Jon to follow through on his agreement to talk to her doctor. By hammering out the details and creating a specific plan of action, Jennifer had taken some control over the situation and ensured Jon's cooperation. Jennifer's use of this communication wonder helped her close the deal and resolve the annoying medical bill problem. Try using this wonder to quickly and easily eliminate miscommunications with others to get the results you want.

COMMUNICATION WONDER

Close the Deal

When you seek someone's cooperation, say,
"I'd like us to work out the specifics of where
we're going from here." Then clarify your
expectations of who is doing what so
you can create accountability for
a specific plan of action.

Rule 13

. . . . .

Save It
for
Later

WHEN I WAS IN COLLEGE I spent a summer working for a company in New York City. Mr. Lewis was my supervisor. Whenever he had something negative to say about my work or anyone else's, he would say it without a moment's hesitation in front of other people in his office, in the elevator, in a conference room or in the hallway. The other two summer interns and I would complain to one another, but never to him. I couldn't understand why this man thought it was okay to put someone down in public. In the end, his criticism had an effect on everyone's behavior, but it wasn't what he intended. When people saw him from a distance walking toward them in the hall, they would instinctively try to get out of his line of vision. Even though he was a difficult man to work for, looking back I have to thank him because he encouraged me to think about criticism and how picking the wrong time to give criticism is pointless and hurtful. Now, because of my former supervisor, I am very aware of where and when I open my mouth to say something critical. Anytime I choose to give criticism, my goal is to have the person listen to me, become aware of what he is doing wrong and then make the appropriate changes. Giving criticism at the wrong time always defeats that purpose.

Mr. Lewis, as well as many other people I have met, was amazingly unaware of the negative effect of criticizing people in public. I hope the stories below will teach you to become more alert to your surroundings when you give criticism. The stories illustrate what happens when criticism is given at the wrong time. Then, you will learn the communication wonder— the rule—for giving criticism at the right time.

My problem with public criticism happened at the office, but Rachel's happened on the athletic field. Rachel told me about her problem after I presented a communication skills seminar for high school students at a leadership conference. Rachel was on the junior varsity soccer team. It was the first game of the season and her father, Mark, came to watch the game. He sat in the stands and cheered her on as the team faced a difficult opponent. In an exciting and intense game, Rachel's team emerged victorious. As soon as the game was over Rachel's father walked over to the sideline where Rachel was standing with her teammates. The team was in a great mood and everyone was joking around, complimenting one another on their victory. Rachel took a moment to introduce her dad to her new friends on the junior varsity team. "Congratulations, you all did a great job," her father announced to his daughter and her friends. "Thanks. I'm glad we were able to pull it off right at the end," one of them responded.

Rachel was happy that her father had come to support her in the first game of the season, but her happiness didn't last long because right after his congratulatory words, her father lowered his voice to give her some constructive criticism. "Rachel," he said, "I noticed that you avoided making long passes during the game. You missed some good opportunities when you didn't kick the ball to girls who were out in the open and able to score. Before the next game you better practice kicking long passes."

Rachel told me that she couldn't believe her father could be so critical of her when her teammates could hear what he was saying. Upset, she looked to her friends to see if they were listening. Even though her father had lowered his voice, Rachel knew that her friends were still able to hear every word he said to her. Rachel was embarrassed and worried that her friends would believe her father's criticism and lose confidence in her ability. Then and there Rachel decided that she would not invite her father to another game because she was afraid of what negative things he might say.

Rachel's father probably had no clue that he had made a communication blunder when he picked the wrong time and the wrong place to share his constructive criticism with his daughter. Lowering his voice to give the criticism didn't help because he still said it around other people who could hear him. Although his criticism might have been helpful if he had given it to his daughter at another time, sharing it with her in public when other people could hear him made it useless, hurtful and upsetting.

Rachel's situation occurred in an informal setting with her father. However, there may be times when you're supposed to give criticism as part of your job responsibilities. You might be the coach or the captain of a team, a teacher, the head of a committee or someone's boss. When you are in such a position, it is especially important not to abuse your power by criticizing someone in public. It is always important to think about where you are and who is listening before you open your mouth to give criticism.

It's Monday morning and your boss, Mr. Friedman, asks you to come to his office for a few minutes. You hesitantly follow him down the hall into his office. You feel like you're in grade school on your way to the principal's office. You're worried about why he suddenly asked to see you. But your worry disappears when Mr. Friedman says, "You're doing a really good job and because of that, I'd like you to lead a team of employees to evaluate ways to improve management-employee communication." You are relieved and actually excited about taking on this leadership role because it is an opportunity to show Mr. Friedman that he is right and that you are an outstanding employee. You think the position might even give you a chance to prove that you should be promoted. After lunch that day you collect the names of four individuals who want to join the committee and e-mail them with the date and time of the first meeting. In the e-mail you ask them to write down their concerns about management-employee communication and give you their lists by the end of the week so you can effectively prepare an agenda for the meeting.

On the day of the meeting, you are ready and eager, but disappointed in Sue, one of the committee members. Sue never submitted her list of concerns to you as you had requested. You hope that she will give you her list at the meeting, or at least offer an explanation for her negligence. You begin the meeting by thanking everyone for their lists. You tell them that you received submissions from everyone but one person. You then look directly at Sue, expecting her to explain, but she doesn't say a word. So you say, "Sue, I didn't receive anything from you. You chose to be on this committee and I was counting on your full participation. You should be a little more responsible. Next time I ask for something, please get it to me on time." With that, Sue quickly scans the room, looking at her colleagues for support, but everyone remains noticeably silent. Self-conscious and very disturbed, she blurts out, "You'll get your list . . . later!"

After the meeting Sue walks straight to your desk. Without hesitation she says, "You know, it's really obvious that your new leadership position has gone to your head. You shouldn't have scolded me like that at the meeting. I volunteered to be on the committee. That should be good enough. And for your information, I didn't have the list for you because my son has been sick. I actually have a lot of suggestions, but you can forget about hearing them because I quit the committee."

You are surprised by Sue's antagonistic response because you don't think you asked for anything out of the ordinary; everyone else turned in a list. But now, because of her reaction, you're wondering whether you handled the situation in the best way. You conclude that you did. It seems clear that Sue overreacted. Being on the committee obviously isn't one of her priorities. You think she should have explained why she didn't submit her list before the meeting. You're glad that you uncovered Sue's unpleasant attitude before she had a chance to slow down the progress of the committee.

You continue working at your desk thinking everything is fine. But is it? No, it's not. You made a communication blunder because you picked the wrong time to criticize Sue when you decided to express your negative thoughts to her in front of her colleagues. As a result, Sue didn't listen to you. Instead of heeding your constructive criticism, Sue became so distressed by your public confrontation that she quit the committee. You lost a valuable participant and alienated a colleague. It shouldn't have ended that way.

COMMUNICATION BLUNDER

Criticizing someone in public while others may be listening is a blunder.

Criticism in public can also have a disastrous effect on a couple's relationship. Can you remember a time when you overheard a husband or wife criticizing his or her spouse in public? It probably made you feel uncomfortable. Can you imagine how the person being criticized must have felt? See what happens when Alan picks the wrong time to criticize his wife.

Alan and Danielle are married and live in Long Island, New York. On this Saturday night they have plans with another couple to have dinner at a great seafood restaurant and then go to a movie. It's 6:15 and they are expecting the other couple to pick them up at their house in fifteen minutes. Danielle, as usual, got home from running errands later than planned. She is now scrambling around the bedroom trying to decide what to wear and looking for a matching black shoe. Ten minutes later Alan shouts up to Danielle, "Our friends will be here in five minutes." "I know," Danielle yells back. "I still have to put on my makeup. When they come, tell them I'll be right there."

Alan is always on time. He hates being late for things and is annoyed with Danielle once again for not planning her day better. Tonight, if Danielle is late, they will have to rush through dinner to get to the movie on time. When Alan hears the car horn honk from the street he shouts to his wife, "They're here. I'm going out to the car. Hurry up." Alan walks out the door and heads to the car. He gets in and tells his friends, "Danielle will be ready in a couple of minutes." While they are waiting for Danielle they talk about the movie they are going to see. Ten minutes into their conversation Alan is feeling irritated with his wife as he and their friends sit in the car waiting for her. At last, he sees her come out of the house and lock the front door.

Danielle gets in the backseat next to her husband and quickly says, "Sorry." Her friends barely hear her words as they begin talking about the fastest way to get to the restaurant. Alan is fuming. He is very angry with his wife for her flippant apology and for making him wait for her all the time. So right there in the car with their friends in the front seats, Alan forcefully says, "Danielle, do you realize that you have a terrible habit of being late? If you planned your day better you wouldn't have been so inconsiderate as to make everyone wait for you." Alan's tone and unexpected comments shock Danielle and their friends. There is an uncomfortable silence in the car until Danielle defensively replies, "Alan, I'm not normally late for things. You don't know what the heck you're talking about." Danielle spends the rest of the car ride ignoring her husband. She decides that she'll wait until she gets home to let him have it for being so rude and embarrassing her in front of their friends.

As the evening progresses Alan realizes that his wife is not talking to him and he begins to wonder why. He thinks back to what he said to her in the car, but convinces himself that he didn't say anything wrong. He knows that it was easy for their friends to excuse her lateness because they don't live with her and they don't have to deal with it as often as he does. Alan is sure that he did the right thing by confronting his wife with the problem when he did because if he waited until later the effect of her lateness might not have been as apparent. Danielle, on the other hand, is thinking, "He's so rude! He didn't have to say those things to me in front of our friends." Danielle was humiliated by Alan's comments and resents him for making her look bad.

What should Alan have done? Alan should have saved his criticism for later. If he had said the same thing but at a different time, when he and Danielle were alone, he could have calmly told Danielle how much her lateness upsets him. Danielle would have had the opportunity to listen to and respond to his comments instead of silently and angrily withdrawing from him. Well-intentioned criticism that is said in public always has the potential to embarrass and humiliate a person, making him or her angry, defensive and hostile.

Whenever you have criticism to share with someone, whether with a friend, a family member or a colleague, it is best to offer your criticism when you are alone with that person and certain that no one else can hear you. Public criticism always makes a situation worse, not better.

COMMUNICATION WONDER

Save It for Later

Save your criticism until you are in a private setting with someone and you are sure that no one else can hear what you're saying.

Rule 14

. . . . .

Make People Your Partners

DO YOU LIKE PEOPLE who tell you what to do? "You have to go to the store right now to get milk," your spouse orders. "You need to do more research on this and get it back to me by the end of the day," your boss demands. "You better be on time," your roommate shouts. Not surprisingly, when people give orders instead of asking you what you would like to do, they sap your motivation and make you angry and resentful. Orders take away your freedom of choice and make you feel powerless. Although you might agree to follow an order once in a while, you probably walk away from the situation disliking the orderer and feeling resistant toward listening to him or her again.

So what does all this mean in the big picture? Does it mean that we should never tell anyone what to do? What about a situation in which a doctor needs to give a patient orders, or a boss needs to tell her employees what to do, or a wife wants to tell her husband to do something for her? Well, the important thing for you to know is that you can get what you want from people without delivering orders. How? By using your power of persuasion. When you order people around, you treat them disrespectfully and provoke resentment. When you use your power of persuasion to offer people choices and listen to their ideas, you motivate them to choose to do something that will be mutually beneficial. Persuasion is an effective way to get someone to *want* to do something for you. By making a small change in your words you can turn an order into a persuasive suggestion so the person feels as though you are on his or her team and you are working together to arrive at a satisfactory outcome. When you create a sense of partnership, you create a winning situation for everyone involved. In the following stories you will learn to identify a communication blunder that can prevent you from getting what you want. Then you will discover the powerful communication wonder that makes others feel good about themselves and motivates them to want to give you what you want.

I remember an experience I had at Harvard in which Kate, the president of a student club, gave the members an order that almost no one followed. At a meeting in May, Kate announced that our club would participate in the annual school Spring Fling, a day of games and food, meant to raise school spirit. The event coordinator had requested that every student club participate in the event in some way by hosting a booth or a game or by selling or collecting tickets. Kate told us,

"Spring Fling is coming up this Saturday and the coordinator of the event called to ask me how our club wanted to participate. I told her we would be happy to collect tickets at the front gate during the event. So everyone should arrive at eleven forty-five on Saturday at the gate near the front lawn. Be ready to collect tickets when the gates open at noon." I wasn't surprised by Kate's authoritative attitude. She was prone to giving orders and today was no different. But I didn't understand why she didn't see the value in finding out what the club members wanted to do at the Spring Fling before responding to the event coordinator. Why did she always seem to feel the need to make decisions without asking other people for their input? Maybe we didn't want to collect tickets. Maybe we would have preferred to host a booth or a game.

I looked around at the other members and could see irritation on their faces. Obviously Kate's attitude had turned them off, too. But it seemed that no one felt like dealing with Kate or making a big deal out of the situation. No one said anything and Kate brought up another topic. Just before we adjourned Kate reminded us, "Don't forget, everyone should be at the front gate at eleven forty-five on Saturday."

When Saturday arrived, although still annoyed with Kate for making a decision without consulting any of us, I walked over to the Spring Fling. There, standing by herself at the front gate, was Kate. "I'm the only one here!" she exclaimed as soon as she saw me. "Why doesn't anyone listen to me? I'm the president of the organization for a reason. I'm supposed to make decisions for the club. Everyone said they would be here to collect tickets and they're not. Now you and I are left with all the responsibility." "Kate," I said, "it's not twelve yet, we still have a few minutes before the gates open. Maybe some more people will show up to help us collect tickets." "Well, they should have been here by now," exclaimed Kate. "I don't understand why people are so unreliable." The minutes passed and no one else from our club arrived at the front gate. Kate and I began collecting tickets. I was annoyed with Kate and Kate was annoyed with everyone else. Kate had no idea that she had made a communication blunder by giving orders instead of asking us what we wanted to do. Although Kate was right about one thing—she was the president and she did have the power to make the final decision on this issue—she showed a lack of respect for us when she didn't ask for our input. Kate didn't realize that giving people orders would not yield the result she wanted. Because she had not involved the members in the decision to collect tickets, they lacked the motivation to follow through on her order.

COMMUNICATION BLUNDER

Ordering someone to do something is a blunder.

Here is an example of how a communication blunder can easily be turned into a communication wonder so you get the results you want. Recently Father Paul, a priest and a good friend of mine, announced publicly for the first time that four years earlier he had been diagnosed with Parkinson's disease. I went to see him to express my concern for his health and to discuss ways that we could collaborate on some projects. When I asked him how he was feeling, he said, "Much better since I started seeing a new doctor a few months ago." "Really," I said, "I'm glad to hear that." "Well," he responded, "before I started with Dr. Golden I was feeling awful. I was taking a lot of medication, but none of it helped. As a matter of fact, I think the side effects of the medicine made me feel even worse. I switched doctors a number of times because I wasn't improving. Eventually I became so distressed by the whole situation that I canceled my doctor's appointments and almost stopped taking my medication. But now, after seeing Dr. Golden, my new neurologist, everything is different. I'm walking a little faster. I can use my left arm, my stomach pains have lessened and my insomnia is nearly nonexistent." I was surprised to hear that one doctor could make such a difference in his life, so I said, "Wow, this doctor sounds like a miracle worker! What did he do for you that made such a remarkable difference?"

"Well, I think it boils down to one specific thing that Dr. Golden said to me," Father Paul responded. "What was that?" I asked. Now my curiosity was at an all-time high. "Well," Father Paul responded, "all the other doctors I saw said the same things to me. At every appointment with a new doctor I would tell him about my symptoms and my diagnosis. Then each doctor would look at my charts and agree that I had Parkinson's disease. At that point, I'd usually sit back and listen to the doctor tell me all about Parkinson's disease and how important it is that I follow his orders relating to which medicines to take, in what amounts and at what time of day. Every doctor would tell me to see a physical therapist and sometimes they would tell me to work less and rest more. Listening to those orders every time overwhelmed and angered me. I felt as though my life was out of control. Gradually, in complete despair, I stopped seeing doctors so I wouldn't have to listen to all of their orders.

"Then, a few months ago something wonderful happened. My friend told me about his cousin who has Parkinson's disease and he gave me the name of his cousin's doctor, who is supposed to be the best. At first I was resistant to seeing another doctor, but eventually because I was feeling so rotten, I agreed to see him, just once. Initially he seemed like all the rest. He asked me to tell him about my condition, which I did. I mentioned every symptom from lack of movement in my left arm to my sleeplessness and stomachaches. When I was exhausted from telling my story for the umpteenth time, I sat back in my chair, prepared to hear the usual set of orders and recommendations. But this time, that didn't happen. The doctor looked at me and said, 'Now that I understand your condition, what do *you* think we should do about it?' I thought I had misunderstood him so I repeated his question, 'Did you say, "What do I think we should do about it?"' 'Yes,' said Dr. Golden. 'What would you like to improve first, your motion, your sleepiness or your stomach pains? I always tackle one problem at a time and I ask my patients to help me design a treatment plan with their specific goals in mind. It is my patients, not me, who have to live with the disease, take the medicine and have the therapy. I would like you to become an active partner in the process of improving your health.'"

Father Paul explained to me, "At first I was stunned by the doctor's question because I had never thought about what I could do to improve my health. I always thought it was the doctor's job to figure that out and tell me what to do. But Dr. Golden helped me realize that it is my life at stake and that I should have a say in my own treatment plan. All the other doctors talked at me, but Dr. Golden talked with me. Because of Dr. Golden's different approach, I experienced an extraordinary burst of energy and hope. After he asked me what I wanted to do, I surprised myself when I blurted out, 'I want to be able to use my left arm again. I want to have less stomach pains. I want to stay awake and have the energy to participate in an entire mass.' Dr. Golden listened to me and then he warmly said, 'Okay then, those are our goals and we'll make them happen together.'

"Dr. Golden and I designed a treatment plan that included the specific times for me to take my pills to correspond with my daily work schedule so that I could get the most benefit from the medication. The plan was aimed at lessening the symptoms of Parkinson's that bothered me most, one at a time. He told me to keep a record of my symptoms and to call him in a week to tell him about any noticeable changes. Over the next week, I rigorously followed the treatment plan and paid close attention to my body. When my symptoms were problematic, I made a record of the time of day and their severity, as Dr. Golden had suggested, so that when I called him I was prepared with the information. He and I discussed my notes and then he suggested that I change the length of time between doses. He explained how this change might reduce the specific side effects that were bothering me. By the end of the second week, I saw a remarkable improvement in my health. Dr. Golden was indeed my miracle worker."

"That's an amazing story," I said. "It seems to me that it all came down to Dr. Golden's method of treating you like a partner, giving you choices and asking you what you wanted to do rather than telling you what you must do. Is that right?" "Yes, that was the big difference," responded Father Paul. "Dr. Golden gave me the opportunity to feel like a participant in my health care decisions. That feeling motivated me to follow through on my treatment plan."

After I left Father Paul's office I thought about how Dr. Golden had masterfully avoided the communication blunder that many other doctors made. Even though Dr. Golden was in a position to give orders, he didn't. He never said, "You must do this"; instead he used a communication wonder to ask his patients questions such as, "What do you think we should do?" He understood the importance of asking his patients questions and giving them choices so that they would be able to participate in their treatment program. Dr. Golden used his power of persuasion to create a partnership with Father Paul that motivated him to like, listen to and cooperate with him so that he would follow his treatment plan. In the short time that Dr. Golden spent with Father Paul, he created a strong and meaningful bond that instilled a sense of optimism in his patient.

By making a small change in your words, you, too, can persuade people to want to do something that will benefit both of you. Whether you are a doctor, a boss, a spouse or someone's boyfriend or girlfriend, it's best to pose questions such as, "What do you think we should do?" or "Do you think you will be able to do this?" instead of making statements such as, "You have to do this," or "You must do this." By asking questions instead of giving orders, you encourage people to cooperate with you so you will have a better chance of getting what you want.

COMMUNICATION WONDER

Make People Your Partners

To get someone's cooperation, offer choices and ask questions such as, "What do you think we should do?" or "Do you think you will be able to do this?"

Rule 15

. . . . .

Acknowledge Others in a New Way

E-MAIL. It is a new style of communication, but one in which the old reliable commonsense principles of communication still apply. The hard part now is to learn how to transfer those old reliable principles of communication to e-mail conversations. One of the most important principles that we must apply to e-mail is simply that effective conversations require back-and-forth communication. For example, when you're in a face-to-face conversation with someone, you talk and he listens, then you listen and he talks. When you ask someone for some information and he calls you the next day or stops by your office to give you the information, you instinctively respond by personally thanking him for his time and effort. Each of these situations is an example of a respectful, back-and-forth pattern of communication. This is just common sense.

Yet this commonsense pattern and principle of communication is often forgotten in the new world of e-mail communication—a world in which written words on a computer screen become your voice. When you have an e-mail conversation, there is no one looking at you or at the other end of the telephone line expecting you to respond. Instead, there is a cold, impersonal machine staring you in the face. As a result, when someone sends you an e-mail and doesn't specifically ask you to respond, you might not think to send a short reply acknowledging that you received it. You might not realize someone is waiting on the end of the computer line to find out whether or not you received his e-mail. In contrast, if you're talking to someone face-to-face or on the phone, you would reply to the person on the spot and acknowledge his comment.

In a sense, in the world of e-mail the reply button is an "acknowledgment button" because it lets the other person know that you received and appreciate his message. By not responding to e-mails, you risk offending and disappointing others. At this point, you still may not believe how important it is to reply to many of the e-mails you receive, but after reading the following stories, you will see that when you fail to write a brief message and click reply, you risk turning yourself into an unlikable person. The communication wonder revealed in this chapter shows you a simple way to persuade friends, family members and colleagues to value you and give you the attention you deserve.

It was Thursday afternoon in December and I had no plans

for the evening, so I was happy to receive this e-mail from my friend Eve: "What are you up to tonight? Want to go out to dinner after work?" I quickly e-mailed her back: "Sure, I'm free for dinner tonight. What time?" A few minutes later she wrote back: "Let's meet at 6:30 P.M. in front of Rockefeller Center on the Fifth Avenue side. We can check out the holiday decorations and then find someplace to eat in the area." That sounded good to me. My plans were settled and I was looking forward to the end of the day.

At 5:30 I had to attend an unexpected meeting at work and I was concerned that it would run past 6:30. Thankfully, it ended at exactly 6:30, which meant I would be only a few minutes late. I quickly went back to my office, grabbed my stuff and headed over to Rockefeller Center to meet Eve. As soon as I saw her I said, "Hi, Eve, sorry I'm a little late. I got stuck in a meeting." "Oh, that's where you've been," she said with annoyance that surprised me. "Eve," I said, looking at my watch, "I'm only ten minutes late." "I don't care about that," she said. "I called you a half hour ago to find out if you were meeting me and you weren't in your office. You know, I wondered if our plans were on and if I should even come. You never confirmed that six-thirty at Rockefeller Center was okay with you, so I wasn't sure that you'd be here." "What?" I asked, bewildered. "Why would you think that? You wrote that we should meet at six-thirty. Obviously, if the time and place weren't good for me, I would have e-mailed you to tell you that. You didn't ask me to reply, so I didn't."

I could tell that my answer didn't make Eve feel any better. "Laurie, I don't know how often you check your e-mail so I wasn't positive you saw my message. Besides, everyone knows that some e-mails get lost in a big black hole. I just wanted a reply from you to confirm our plans. It wasn't nice of you to leave me hanging like that."

Eve made a good point. As soon as I received her e-mail with the time and place to meet I was satisfied because I had all the information I needed. As far as I was concerned, our e-mail communication was over. I didn't see the need to send Eve a reply, especially since she didn't ask me to confirm anything. But by not replying I unnecessarily stressed Eve out and annoyed her. When I thought about what I had done, common sense told me that I made a communication blunder. If Eve and I had made plans over the phone and she said, "Let's meet at six-thirty," I would have responded to her at that moment by saying something like, "That sounds great. See you later." But because I was using the computer to communicate, I didn't realize that she was waiting for me to respond. So I made a communication blunder when I failed to acknowledge her e-mail by clicking the reply button and sending a short message to confirm our plans.

It's important to remember that sending a reply to an e-mail, even when it is not requested, is an important and meaningful last step in a two-way communication. One day, when I was in the middle of writing a legal research memo, I received an e-mail from Michael, my co-counsel in a case. He was writing a brief due the next day and he asked me to do him a favor. He wrote: "I'm not in my office today and I'm finishing up the brief that's due tomorrow. I hope you don't mind, but would you please e-mail me copies of the briefs relating to the case so that I can review them again tonight at home."

Truthfully, I wasn't eager to do the favor for him because I was very busy and the briefs weren't in my office. It would take me a while to get them and scan them into the computer system. But Michael really needed them and I wanted to be helpful, so I wrote back: "Okay, I'll do it. I'll e-mail the briefs to you but it's going to take a little while to locate the files. I'll send them to you within the hour."

I went down to the records department to find the briefs. After I had collected and scanned them into the computer system, I went back to my office and wrote a short e-mail that said: "Michael, here are the briefs you requested. Good luck with your writing." I attached the briefs to the e-mail and clicked send. Then I went back to writing my legal research memo. Every so often I found myself looking up at my computer screen, anticipating a reply e-mail from Michael. I had spent time getting him the information that he wanted and I wasn't sure the large attachments would go through. If they had gone through, I hoped that Michael would acknowledge that he had received them and thank me for my time. I didn't hear from Michael again that day so I assumed he had received the e-mail because I would have heard from him if he hadn't. I thought it was inconsiderate of Michael not to reply to let me know that he had received the documents. It appeared to me that once Michael got the briefs that he wanted, he never gave me a second thought. Although I didn't think that Michael was a bad person for ignoring me, I did think his lack of response was thoughtless.

Michael made a communication blunder when he didn't reply to my e-mail. He may not have thought he needed to reply because I didn't ask him to. But his indifference to me made me feel unappreciated and less inclined to want to help him out in the future. Michael didn't realize that by ignoring someone's e-mail he is essentially ignoring and offending that person.

COMMUNICATION BLUNDER

It is a blunder to assume that you don't
need to reply to an e-mail because
the sender didn't ask you to.

The following story is another example of how you can create negative feelings when you don't reply to an e-mail. My friend Michelle called to tell me some exciting news. "Laurie," she said, "you won't believe what I just did! You know how I've been talking about getting a dog? Well, I just walked into a pet store and spontaneously bought a cocker spaniel! I'm back home with him now and I'm so excited. I'm going to spend this vacation learning to take care of him. He's so little and so cute, you have to come over to see him." Her enthusiasm was contagious, so during my lunch break that day I headed straight to Michelle's apartment to see her new dog.

When I arrived, Michelle was on the phone with one of our friends, Stacey, who also recently bought a dog. Michelle was saying, "Stacey, since you're home today, I'll take some digital photos of my dog and e-mail them to you so you can see for yourself how cute he is! But I have to go now. Laurie just got here." They ended their conversation and Michelle turned to me and said, "Thanks for coming over. Isn't he precious? Can you believe I finally got a dog?" "No, it's hard to believe," I replied. "He is so adorable and tiny! What are you going to name him?" "I'm naming him Harry," Michelle said. We both sat down on the floor to play with Harry. "You know

what," Michelle said, "let's take the digital photos of him now
so I can e-mail them to Stacey. I'll hold Harry while you take
the pictures." I took pictures of Harry in Michelle's lap and
then of Harry playing with his new toys. Then Michelle got up
and went directly to her computer to e-mail the pictures to
Stacey.

About a half hour later I had to leave to get back to my office, so I told Michelle I would try to stop by her apartment
the next day after work to see if she needed help with anything. When I arrived the next day, Michelle was still confident that she had made the right decision to get a dog. "I
e-mailed the pictures of Harry to my brother," Michelle said.
"He loved them and can't wait to come over next week to see
him." "By the way," I wondered aloud, "what did Stacey say
about the pictures?" "You know, I never heard from Stacey
and I'm annoyed," Michelle said. "When she got her dog, I
was so happy and excited for her that I volunteered to dog-sit
for a few days when she had to go on a business trip. It's just
plain rude of her not to reply to my e-mail. It reminds me of
how self-centered she can be. I'm sure she would have replied
to my e-mail if I had taken pictures of her dog and e-mailed
them to her!" Michelle was clearly offended and disappointed
in Stacey because she hadn't replied to her e-mail. I asked
Michelle, "Did you ask Stacey to reply to your e-mail when
you sent it to her?" "No," Michelle said. "Why should I? She
should know that she should respond. I took the time to take
the photos and send them to her. Don't you think it would
have been nice if she took a minute to send me a reply?"

Stacey made a communication blunder and offended
Michelle when she didn't reply to her e-mail. Stacey didn't re-

alize that the principles of communication that apply to face-to-face communication also apply to people communicating in the hi-tech world of e-mail. If Michelle had shown Stacey the photos in person, Stacey undoubtedly would have commented on them. Therefore, when Michelle sent Stacey the pictures via e-mail, Stacey should have known that it was appropriate to reply, even though she wasn't asked to. All human beings want and deserve to hear words of acknowledgment, appreciation and praise, so it's not surprising that Michelle was hurt and disappointed by her friend's lack of attention and recognition. Stacey should have used the communication wonder for effective e-mail communication. Here's the key: When Stacey received the e-mail from Michelle, she should have replied automatically to Michelle to let her know that she had received it, and more important, to comment on her new dog.

This communication wonder of automatically replying to an e-mail should become a habit for you, too. Of course, that's not to say that you need to reply to things like newsletters, mass mailings and random e-mails from people you don't know. Remember, it never hurts to send someone you know a reply, but it can be destructive and offensive when you don't. The next time you check your e-mail and find a message with information, a joke, pictures, an article or a card from someone you know, be sure to acknowledge it with an e-mail reply. This wonder will prove to be an effective and valuable rule for you to follow to build and reinforce relationships with your friends, family members and colleagues.

•   •   •   •   •

COMMUNICATION WONDER

Acknowledge Others in a New Way

Make it a habit to reply to e-mail messages
you receive, so that the senders
are sure you have read them.

Rule 16

· · · · ·

Show You
Care

I'LL BET YOU'VE HEARD this before: Listening is a crucial part of communication. When you listen to someone you show him that you value him and what he has to say. In turn, he values you and what you have to say. Now here is something new to consider. It's one thing to listen, but it's quite another thing to listen, remember and follow up on what you've heard. Following up means remembering to ask someone about something important to him that he told you earlier. When you follow up, you instantly tell that person that he is important to you because you're thinking about him, and in turn, you become important to him. In fact, when you forget to follow up you tell that person just the opposite—that you don't care about him and he is not important to you. It may seem difficult to know how and when to follow up on something effectively, but the amazing thing is that it becomes easy once you learn the simple rule in this chapter.

In the stories below you will see how people overlook meaningful opportunities to connect with other people. Then you will discover the communication wonder that gives you the right words to say at the right time to the right person so that you connect with others and strengthen relationships.

One Thursday evening in late March, Paul calls his friend John. "Hi, John, it looks like golf season is upon us! Have you heard the weather report for this weekend? It's supposed to be unusually nice on Saturday. Probably warm enough for us to get out on the golf course. Do you want to play eighteen holes?" "I wish I could," John says, "but I'll probably need the day to rest." "Why do you have to rest?" Paul asks. "Well, I'm scheduled for a colonoscopy late Friday afternoon so I don't think I'll be in the mood to play golf Saturday morning." "Oh," says Paul, who isn't sure how to respond to that information. "Can I ask you, why do you need a colonoscopy?" "During my last general physical exam my doctor noticed something unusual so he strongly suggested that I schedule a colonoscopy as soon as possible. Over the years I've avoided taking the test for the obvious reasons, but now it seems I no longer have a choice. I'm really worried about this test because my uncle died from colon cancer last year and if I remember correctly he found out about it when he had a colonoscopy. I just hope I haven't waited too long to take the test." "Well, you shouldn't make yourself sick worrying about it. I'm sure everything will be fine. Most often things like this turn out to be nothing," offers Paul. "I hope you're right. In any event, have a good time on the golf course."

John has the colonoscopy on Friday. Fortunately everything is fine. After the weekend, John receives a call from Paul. John assumes Paul is calling to find out how he is feeling and the results of his medical test, but Paul doesn't ask him anything about it. In fact, Paul's only reason for calling is to set up a golf game. He asks John, "Do you want to play golf on Sunday? I'll find a couple of guys to make it a foursome." John thinks a moment and agrees to play golf with Paul. They decide to meet at the golf course for a 9 A.M. tee-off time, which Paul says he'll arrange. John hangs up and thinks, "I can't believe Paul didn't ask me about the results of my colonoscopy. He knew how worried I was about it. Until now, I never realized that Paul is so preoccupied with himself. He never forgets to arrange golf games. I'm hurt that he hasn't given me a second thought. I guess I'm just a golf friend, not a real friend like I thought I was."

Paul made a communication blunder, not because he said something wrong but because he didn't say enough. Paul didn't intentionally insult his friend. He simply forgot that John had had a medical test the previous week. When John originally told him about the test, Paul didn't register it in his head as something important to remember. Paul didn't realize that what is important to someone he cares about should also be important to him. By not calling John to find out the results of his medical test, Paul missed a significant opportunity to show John that their friendship matters to him.

COMMUNICATION BLUNDER

When a person tells you something that is important to him, it is a blunder if you don't follow up on it with him in a timely manner.

In the next story, about Dina and Sandra, we will explore this communication blunder in more detail and you will learn the communication wonder you should use to strengthen relationships with friends, family members and colleagues.

One Saturday afternoon Dina and Sandra, two single women who've been friends for many years, are having coffee together at a café. Dina is particularly preoccupied and anxious because she has a blind date that evening. "I'm so nervous," she announces to Sandra. "This is the first guy I've gone out with who I met over the Internet. We only talked on the phone once to set up the dinner date. We e-mailed back and forth a few times and I saw his picture on the website, but how can I trust a picture? He looks attractive, but pictures can be deceiving, as can people, for that matter. I don't know why I'm doing this. If this date doesn't go well, then I'm done with Internet dating forever." "Hey, don't be so negative about it," Sandra responds. "You have to take chances in your life. Maybe this guy will be great or maybe he'll be ugly and boring! But no matter what, just keep in mind, it's only a date. I'm sure you can survive being with someone you don't like for one evening." "I guess so," responds Dina. They chat about other things for an hour or so, then say their good-byes and head their separate ways.

Dina goes on her blind date that night and, surprisingly, she has a good time. At the end of the evening she and her date make plans to see each other again the following weekend. Dina can't wait to tell Sandra about how well her date went. She figures that Sandra will be curious about her date and call her the next day to find out what happened. When Dina doesn't hear from Sandra by Thursday, Dina figures that Sandra has probably been too busy, so she calls her to tell her about the date.

"Hi, Sandra, how are you doing?" Sandra immediately blurts out, "Dina, I'm so glad it's you. You couldn't have picked a better time to call. My mom and I got into an argument this morning and I can't figure out what to do. I could use your help." Sandra proceeds to give Dina the details about the argument with her mother. As Sandra talks all about herself and her mother, Dina feels ignored and frustrated.

Before Sandra is finished, Dina interrupts. "Listen, Sandra, you know I would be happy to hear about your problem with your mother, but how about showing some interest in my life? Don't you remember that I had a blind date last weekend that I was really nervous about? You never took a minute to call me to find out how it went and now when I call you, all you do is talk about yourself and your mother. Are you that busy that you don't have time for your friends?" "Okay, I'm sorry. So how was your date?" "It went better than I expected. He was really nice and he actually looked like his picture. I'm going to see him again on Friday night." "Oh," Sandra responds unenthusiastically, without asking any questions to encourage Dina to talk more about her date. Dina quickly recognizes that she's not going to get the feedback and attention she wants from Sandra, so she says, "It seems to me that this is not a good time for you. Why don't you solve your problem with your mother and give me a call when you're less distracted?" "Okay, I suppose that's a good idea." After hanging up, Sandra can't imagine why Dina is so upset with her just because she didn't call to find out about her blind date. Sandra thinks to herself, "If anyone should be upset it should be me because of the problem I'm having with my mother."

Sandra doesn't realize that Dina would have been happy to help her solve her problem with her mother, if Sandra had shown an interest in her by asking about her date. Not only did Sandra not remember to follow up on Dina's date by calling to find out how it went, when Dina called Sandra, all Sandra did was talk about her own situation. Dina interpreted Sandra's indifference to her date as indifference to her and their friendship.

Sandra should have taken advantage of the opportunity to follow up on the date and show her friend that she cares about what is going on in her life. She should have made a point of calling her friend after her blind date to specifically ask, "How was your date?" That would have opened up the lines of communication necessary to keep a relationship alive and strong. If Sandra was worried she would forget to follow up, she could easily have put a note in her datebook or calendar or even on her refrigerator that said: "Sunday—follow up on Dina's date." By remembering to follow up on Dina's blind date, Sandra would have instantly let Dina know that she is important to her and Dina would have been happy to take an interest in Sandra's life.

Whenever someone tells you about something personal that is important to him, such as a doctor's appointment, an interview, a daughter's wedding, a date or a special event, make it a priority to follow up on it with that person in a future conversation. This communication wonder works with your clients and customers as well. It takes only one follow-up call to bring you closer to someone you care about.

COMMUNICATION WONDER

Show You Care

When someone tells you something that is important to him, make a point of following up on it with that person.

Rule 17

. . . . .

Give a Final Answer

HAVE YOU EVER SAID to someone, "I'll see what I can do" or "I might be available," or "I'll try to get it for you," and then when you found out that you couldn't do it or you weren't available, you stopped thinking about the situation and never got back to the person to tell him or her the result? Although this may not seem like a big deal, it is to the person who is left in a position of uncertainty. When someone expects a response from you and never receives it, you instantly persuade that person to become irritated and angry with you. When you leave someone hanging, without giving him or her a final answer, you set the stage for miscommunication, frustration and disappointment.

My friend Sheila quickly lost interest in Todd, a man she was dating, because he left her in a position of uncertainty. Sheila met Todd at a friend's party one Friday night and they hit it off right away. She gave him her phone number and a few days later he called to ask her out. The next weekend they had dinner together. After Todd dropped her off at her apartment Sheila thought, "Finally, I met a man who is interesting, sincere and attractive, and I actually want to go out with him again. I hope he calls me." Then, just as Sheila had hoped, the following Monday night Todd called her. She was excited to hear his voice. Sheila assumed he was calling to make plans for a second date. But that didn't quite happen. Instead, he said, "Sheila, I want to see you this weekend but I may have a problem. I have a friend coming into town who might be staying with me for the weekend. I'm going to call him and try to get him to stay with another friend of ours. If that works out, do you want to go out Saturday night?" "Sure," Sheila answered, happy that Todd had called so soon after their first date. They talked for a while, then right before they hung up Todd said, "If Saturday night doesn't work out, let's try for the following weekend." "Okay," Sheila responded.

When Sheila came home from work the next evening, she was looking forward to Todd's phone call. She hoped he would tell her that he had arranged things so that they could see each other on Saturday night. But Todd didn't call. Sheila figured that Todd would most certainly call her the next evening to let her know what was going on that weekend. But that didn't happen either. When Wednesday night came and went and Sheila still hadn't heard from him, she became annoyed. She thought, "If Todd is really as sincere as he seemed, he would have called me by now to give me an update." When Sheila didn't hear from Todd on Thursday night, she assumed they weren't going out on Saturday. She became incredibly irritated with him for not having the decency to call her to tell her he couldn't see her. She considered calling him but decided against it because she didn't want to give him the impression that she was running after him. So Friday at work, Sheila decided to make other plans. She called two of her friends to find out what they were doing Saturday night, only to discover that each of them already had a date. Sheila was furious with herself for keeping Saturday night open as long as she did and for relying on Todd for her plans. Now, because of Todd's inconsiderate behavior and her own stupidity, she would be home alone on Saturday night.

The following Tuesday, Todd surprised Sheila with a phone call. "Hi, how was your weekend?" he asked cheerfully, as if nothing was wrong. Sheila couldn't believe the upbeat inflection in his voice after he had been so rude to her. "My weekend?" repeated Sheila, who instantly decided to pretend that she had enjoyed a great weekend in spite of him. "It was fantastic. How was your weekend?" "Oh, it was nice. I had a good time hanging out with my friend in New York. We visited Ellis Island and the Statue of Liberty. So tell me, do you want to have dinner this Saturday night?" "Dinner with you?" Sheila asked in disbelief. "Todd, don't you think it was inconsiderate of you not to call me to let me know what was happening this past Saturday night? You said you would try to arrange things with your friend so that we could get together and then I never heard from you again." "What?" responded Todd, becoming defensive. "I never said I would get back to you. All I said was that I would try to get my friend to stay somewhere else. As it turned out, he needed to stay with me. I assumed

you would know that since I didn't call, I couldn't see you."
"Todd, I did realize that you couldn't see me, but I didn't like
waiting for your call wondering whether our plans were on or
off. I'm just curious, when exactly did you find out that your
friend was definitely staying with you?" "Let me think," Todd
answered hesitantly. "I talked to him the night after I talked to
you. That would be Tuesday." Now that really pushed Sheila's
buttons. "So then," Sheila responded, "while you knew on Tuesday that we couldn't see each other on Saturday, you never
bothered to call me. Don't you think it was rude to leave me
dangling like that?" "Listen," Todd said, annoyed with Sheila's
third degree, "I didn't mean to upset you. I just didn't think
about it. Besides, you should have made other plans when I
didn't get back to you."

Sheila couldn't believe that Todd was defending his actions
and refused to admit that he had been rude. The more he
talked, the more his words angered her and persuaded her to
dislike him. Sheila no longer had any interest in talking to or
seeing him so she said, "Todd, I have to go now and I already
have plans for this weekend." All Todd could say was, "Okay."
Sheila hung up the phone upset and disappointed. She
thought to herself, "How could Todd not admit that he was
wrong and that he should have called me, especially after I
told him how I felt?" She was too angry with him to see him
that weekend or maybe ever again.

How did this communication blunder happen? The answer
is simple. When Todd found out that his friend needed to stay
with him, he was satisfied because he knew exactly what his
plans were for the weekend. He didn't think about Sheila or
the fact that she was waiting for him to call to tell her his
plans so she would know their tentative date for Saturday

night was off. Even after Sheila had told him that she was annoyed with him for leaving her dangling, without giving her a final answer, Todd still didn't get it and continued to defend his actions. He didn't realize he should have called Sheila back even though he didn't say he would.

COMMUNICATION BLUNDER

It is a blunder to assume that it is not necessary to get back to someone with a final answer after you tell that person "I'll try" or "maybe."

Here's a chance to see this same communication blunder happen in the workplace. Peter, a friend of my father's, owned a lamp manufacturing company in New York that also imported lamps from China. He sold his products to wholesalers who sold them to retailers. Customers often called Peter directly when they wanted him to speed up delivery of a foreign order. One Monday morning, Peter received an unexpected call from Sam, one of his bigger customers. "Peter, remember when I ordered four thousand pieces of number 122006 lamp to be delivered right after New Year's? Well, I must have them sooner. Some customers called to tell me that the lamp is hot and they want a supply in their stores before Christmas. But here's the problem. I don't have any left in my warehouse to ship to them. Peter, you have to do something to speed up my delivery."

Peter frequently received requests like this and they always created enormous pressure for him. He ran a successful business and worked hard to satisfy his customers' needs. But dealing with the factories in China was always difficult, especially when it came to shipping dates. So Peter explained, "Sam, I understand your problem, but speeding up a delivery is difficult. The factory in China that manufactures those lamps is known for its high-quality merchandise so they're extremely busy, especially at this time of year. They generally have a large backlog of orders so they're seldom able to speed anything up. And even if we could get the factory to complete your order early, it would still take four weeks to arrive by boat in the United States." "But, Peter, with all the business I give you and you give them, can't you get some special attention?" Sam asked in frustration. "If you could just get the factory to rush production so that the lamps are ready for shipment two weeks earlier, I'd get them before Christmas and everything would be fine. I'm only asking for two weeks." "Well," Peter replied, trying to think of something to say that would satisfy Sam so he could get off the phone, "you did agree to accept your delivery at the beginning of the new year, so that's what you should expect. But I will call the factory in China to try to push them to expedite your order. But I doubt it will help." "Okay," said Sam, who now seemed a little more hopeful, believing that Peter understood his problem and was going to try to help him out.

Because of the time difference, Peter had to wait until later that evening to call his supplier in China. As expected, Peter was unable to get the factory to move up the shipping date. He didn't call Sam back because he didn't have anything new to tell him. Besides, Peter was sure Sam would assume that nothing good had been accomplished by his call to China.

A week later, Sam called Peter again. "I haven't heard from

you. What happened? No news is good news, right? You did do something to speed up my order, didn't you?" "Oh," said Peter, instantly realizing that he had made a mistake by not getting back to Sam. "I'm sorry. I called the factory in China, but as expected, they can't change the shipping date." "What?" exclaimed Sam. "I've been telling my customers that it's possible they will have the lamps in their stores before Christmas." "Sam, I didn't tell you that I would be able to do that for you. I only said I would try, which I did, but unsuccessfully." Sam became even more frustrated. "Peter, why didn't you at least call me to tell me that? For the past week I've been going around thinking that the factory might be rushing my order. You misled me by not calling me. Then I misled my customers by telling them that a pre-Christmas delivery was possible. I'm very disappointed."

Peter made a serious communication blunder by not getting back to Sam with a final answer. He neglected to call Sam back with the information that would have eliminated the uncertainty surrounding the delivery date. Peter assumed that Sam would know that nothing positive had resulted from his phone call to China when he didn't call him back to tell him otherwise. Unfortunately, Sam and Peter interpreted the words "I'll try" differently. To Sam "I'll try" meant "Yes, I may be able to help you." Whereas to Peter "I'll try" meant "No, I can't help you unless you hear from me." This communication blunder caused a rift in their working relationship.

Peter should have used a communication wonder and called Sam back to say that he had tried to arrange an earlier shipping date but couldn't. By getting back to Sam, even with bad news, Peter would have had an opportunity to show Sam that he is a person who can be trusted to follow through on his commitments. Although Sam would not have been happy with Peter's answer, he would have become aware of Peter's conscientiousness and the effort he had made to try to help him. Peter's return phone call also would have enabled Sam to give his customers an accurate delivery date.

Whenever you hear yourself telling someone "I'll try," assume that the person thinks you *can* do it, unless you specifically get back to him to tell him you can't. Think of the communication wonder in this way: Once the words "I'll try" come out of your mouth, you are obligated to let that person know the positive or negative result of your "trying." Getting back to people is a simple way to persuade them that you are a reliable and trustworthy person.

COMMUNICATION WONDER

Give a Final Answer

When you say "I'll try" to someone, it is your obligation to get back to that person with the results of your "trying."

Rule 18

. . . . .

Prepare
Your
Evidence

WHEN YOU WALK INTO a job interview you most likely have prepared yourself to be persuasive. You have the answers ready to potential questions such as, "Why do you want this job?" "Why should I hire you?" and "What is your best asset?" You arrive with a mental list of your prior experiences that highlight the skills that make you qualified for the position. You are eager to prove to the interviewer that you are perfect for the job. With your evidence in hand you are ready to speak confidently, enthusiastically and persuasively.

It's obvious that preparing evidence to support your position is crucial in a job interview and in a courtroom. But what is less obvious is that preparing evidence is also an integral part of everyday conversations in which you want something from someone or you want someone to agree with you. People need to hear your reasons and evidence to understand your position and be persuaded to arrive at the conclusion you want. In the following stories you will see how lack of preparation is a communication blunder. Then you will see how taking the time to prepare your evidence before opening your mouth instantly increases your chances of persuading someone to cooperate with you.

David is at home one evening watching television with his wife, Marion. During a commercial break he tells her that he's upset with his brother Roger and sister-in-law Karen. "Why are you upset?" Marion asks. "Well, I spoke to my mother yesterday and she mentioned Roger's fiftieth birthday party. Apparently it's at a restaurant in Manhattan a week from Saturday." "Really? This is the first I've heard of it. What else did you find out?" David continued, "My mom's flying up from Florida just for the party. She assumed that we were invited. This morning when Roger called me, I was sure he was calling to invite us to the party, but when he didn't say a word about his birthday I got really upset. Are you sure Karen didn't call you last week to tell you about it?" "I'm positive. I haven't talked to her in weeks," replied Marion, who continued, "Is it possible that they mailed the invitations and ours got lost?" "No, my mother said they called everyone to invite them because Roger and Karen made their plans for the party too late to print invitations and send them out. It's hard to believe that he didn't invite us. I'm so disappointed," remarked David. "You're disappointed? I'm angry. Nothing your brother does surprises me. He's always been inconsiderate and selfish. David, you have to talk to him about this. I know we're not close to him, but we should have been invited. We're family," declared Marion. "You're right," David emphatically agreed. "We've always been there for him whenever he needed our help and now he has the nerve to ignore us. If it's true that we're not invited, then he should know that we're offended and he should apologize."

All riled up, David jumped up from the couch and headed to the kitchen to call his brother. Marion turned down the volume on the TV so she could hear what David said. Roger answered and they greeted each other. Then David explained the reason for his call. "I talked to Mom yesterday and she told me that you're having a birthday party and you called everyone to invite them. Unless I'm mistaken, Marion and I haven't been invited and I don't understand why." There was sudden silence on the phone. Then Roger said something that made David angry. "David, you're right. I didn't invite you and Marion. I'm only having a small party—about twenty people. The party is for my friends, not family. You have to admit that we're not really friends. We seldom socialize with each other." "What does that have to do with it?" David exclaimed. "I'm your brother and I should have been invited. You invited Mom, she's family, so how can you say that you didn't invite any family?" "I invited Mom because I felt like I had no choice." "Well, as I see it," David said, "you didn't have a choice with me either, not if you care about me." Roger responded, "David, it's only a party. Don't make such a big deal out of it."

Each of Roger's excuses reverberated in David's head. David didn't know what else to say to prove to Roger that he had done something wrong, so he blurted out, "Roger, I've always been there for you as a brother. You should start acting like a brother to me. You hurt my feelings and insulted me by not inviting me to your party. Don't you think that's wrong?" "David, you don't know what you're talking about. When have you been there for me?" Roger demanded. David would have liked to respond with strength and confidence, but he didn't know what to say. Suddenly on the defensive, he couldn't think of an example of how he'd been there for his brother, so he announced, "Roger, I don't need to give you a list. You know exactly what I mean. Look, I don't want to get into a fight about this. Why don't you just think about what you did and call me when you're ready to apologize." Roger quickly responded, "You're making a mountain out of a molehill. This is just a little party." David couldn't deal with Roger's selfishness and stubbornness anymore. "Roger, I'm hanging up now. I have nothing more to say to you."

David hung up and walked back into the den seething. He repeated the conversation to Marion and added, "That phone call was absolutely useless. Roger doesn't understand how I feel and I couldn't get my thoughts together fast enough to explain myself. I think I made the situation worse." Marion also thought David could have handled the situation better. She said, "David, when Roger said you didn't do anything for him you should have reminded him that we invited him and his wife to our small anniversary party six months ago even though we don't socialize with them. Don't you remember we had a conversation about whether or not to invite them? We decided it was the right thing to do because they are family and we didn't want to hurt their feelings." "Oh, you're so right. I should have reminded him of that," David said, gritting his teeth. Marion went on, "And you should have reminded him how we were there for him when he was getting divorced a few years ago. Don't you remember how he spent so much time in our house telling us about his problems? We patiently listened to him and tried to be supportive." "Yes, I should have said that, too. Why didn't you remind me of those things before I called Roger?" "You didn't ask me. You just got up and went to call him." "Oh, well," David said, "if the situation arises, I'll be sure to remind him of the things you just said. You know, now that we're talking about it, I can think of a lot of other things I should have said to my brother."

David was aware that he could have handled the situation better. He made a communication blunder when he called without preparing his evidence for why he should receive an apology. David had expected that once Roger understood that he was offended Roger would quickly apologize. But that didn't happen. David's vague and unsubstantial comments didn't help his brother see things from his perspective. As a result, David's conversation with his brother spun out of control and only made the situation worse.

COMMUNICATION BLUNDER

It is a blunder to jump into a conversation without preparation when you want something specific or you want someone to agree with you.

Here is an example of how this blunder plays out in the workplace. My friend Sarah was a sportswear merchandising assistant in the corporate office of a clothing chain. After about a year in her job she started complaining to me about work. Her supervisor, Danielle, had been promoted and replaced by a woman named Martha. Until this change in management, Sarah had enjoyed her job, but she was upset with her new supervisor because she felt underutilized. She used to spend part of her day attending product selection meetings where changes in clothing trends, new products and catalog placements were discussed. The rest of her day was spent doing paperwork, which included filling out order forms, updating inventory lists and reviewing catalogs for accuracy. Sarah and her former supervisor used to share the paperwork so they could both participate in the meetings and keep up on the trends.

Sarah was content with the division of labor until Martha, overly confident and aggressive, arrived on the scene. Martha, who felt paperwork was not part of her job, gave Sarah total responsibility for it. For weeks Sarah was overworked and angry with Martha because she no longer had time to attend the meetings where she could learn about the latest market trends. At first Sarah hoped the change in her job responsibilities would be temporary, but after talking to Martha about it she knew it wasn't. Sarah decided to talk to Stephen, the department manager, to see if he could remedy the situation.

The day after her meeting with Stephen, I called Sarah to follow up and find out what had happened. She told me about her conversation with Stephen and asked me to help her figure out what she said wrong. Sarah had been nervous when she knocked on Stephen's office door. He invited her in and asked, "What's on your mind?" Sarah began to explain the situation. She said, "I'm not happy with the change in my job responsibilities since Martha took over as department supervisor. When Danielle was supervisor we shared the paperwork so that we both had time to attend the product selection meetings.

But now that Martha's on board, I don't have time to go to the meetings, because Martha designated me to do the paperwork full-time and it's not working out. I should be attending the product selection meetings because I learn so much at them. I spoke to Martha about the problem, but she doesn't see a need for change. I was hoping that you would be able to do something about this." Sarah felt proud of herself for taking charge of the situation and speaking up.

But Stephen's response quickly destroyed her optimism. "Sarah, first of all, I read your evaluation and I want to compliment you on doing an excellent job, whether you're doing paperwork or participating in product selection meetings. You're an extremely conscientious employee. But from what you just said, I think Martha's idea is a good one. I don't think it makes sense to split up the paperwork. It would be a waste of time for the two of you to divide up your workload every day. Besides, that approach would definitely leave room for error." Sarah was shocked by his response. She hadn't expected him to take Martha's side. Sarah didn't know what else to say so she repeated herself. "But Danielle and I used to divide up the paperwork and it worked out fine." Stephen, apparently unconvinced, said, "I'll talk to Martha to see what I can do. Sarah, you should remember that you can't always have everything you want. Sometimes you have to do things that you don't want to do, especially if you want to move up the ladder of success." This comment instantly infuriated Sarah, but she didn't want to create a conflict with her boss, so she just said, "Okay, please talk to Martha." Then she got up and walked out of Stephen's office. Sarah blamed herself for the negative outcome of their conversation. Stephen basically told her she would have to live with the situation. Sarah knew she hadn't been very persuasive and she had little confidence that his "talk" with Martha would change anything. In fact, Sarah was concerned that Martha would become angry with her for going to Stephen. What a mess this whole thing had turned out to be. Sarah told me that she wished she had kept her mouth shut.

Where did Sarah go wrong? Sarah didn't know the 3 R's of Instant Persuasion—how to say the Right thing at the Right time to the Right person. In this situation Sarah made a communication blunder by walking into Stephen's office to present her position without preparing her evidence. When Stephen didn't respond the way Sarah expected him to, she became flustered and didn't know what else to say, so she repeated herself. Sarah expected Stephen to be persuaded by her sincerity and hard work. But he wasn't. Stephen, like everyone else, needed to have solid evidence to persuade him to make a change in her daily work schedule.

Sarah should have used a communication wonder. She should have prepared the evidence she needed to back up her position and persuade Stephen to agree with her. By preparing her evidence in advance, Sarah would have had the confidence to direct the conversation instead of letting Stephen take control of it and direct her. Sarah made the following vague and unpersuasive comment to Stephen—"I should be attending the product selection meetings because I learn so much at them." Sarah should have been prepared to back up that statement with specific reasons why attending the meetings is important. For example, Sarah could have said: (1) "I would be able to write the new purchase orders at the meeting and not have to wait for Martha to pass on the information to me"; (2) "I would gain valuable knowledge about how to price merchandise and anticipate future trends so I could do a better job for the company"; and (3) "When I took this job the job description for merchandising assistant included attending product development meetings and the paperwork connected to ordering merchandise."

By preparing her evidence in advance and bringing a list of those points with her to the meeting with Stephen, Sarah would have impressed and influenced him with her well-thought-out position. She would have shown herself to be a credible and responsible employee whose concerns should be taken seriously.

Preparing your evidence in advance is a simple way to instantly become more persuasive and confident when you speak to friends, family members and colleagues. Anytime you want to persuade someone to give you something or to agree with you, offer solid reasons to support your request. With a little forethought, you might be surprised at your accomplishments.

COMMUNICATION WONDER

Prepare Your Evidence

Before you attempt to persuade someone to give you something or to agree with you, prepare a list of specific reasons to support your request.

Rule 19

· · · · ·

Get Off
the
Hook

YOU KNOW THAT FEELING. I know that feeling. We all know that feeling. It's that feeling of guilt mixed with stress and anxiety. It hits you the moment someone you like asks you for a favor that you don't want to do.

A friend asks to borrow your car, but you know that he isn't the best driver and you don't want to lend it to him. What do you say to your friend? You could simply say, "No. I don't want to lend you my car." But if you answer that way, you can expect that your friend won't be satisfied because you didn't give him a reason for your refusal. In a situation like this, you can expect your friend's next question to be, "Why won't you lend me your car?" Now you're stuck in a real bind. If you tell him the truth—that you don't trust him with it—you will offend him and create antagonism between the two of you. So what do you do to solve this dilemma? You could try an excuse. You could tell him that you need your car on the day he wants to borrow it. But if you use an excuse, then it's possible that your friend will ask you for the same favor the following week and you would be stuck all over again.

There is a third choice, which is to agree to do the favor despite your reservations. But this choice is not any better than the first two because if you say yes to the favor, you will probably be angry with yourself and resent your friend for imposing on you.

So what do you do when someone asks you for a favor and neither a yes nor a no answer works to create a solution that satisfies both of you? Well, that's the perfect time to employ the "get off the hook" communication wonder. This wonder is a quick and simple way to get what you want with the certainty and courtesy that will persuade someone to respect your answer. In this chapter, I show you how saying the wrong thing at the wrong time can weaken a relationship. Then I reveal the empowering words you can say at the right time to keep your foot out of your mouth and resolve this unique and difficult dilemma in the best possible way.

I remember an incident that happened many years ago between two of my roommates during my first year in college. One evening when we were all going out to a party, my roommate Michelle couldn't find anything to wear. Her closet was full of clothes, but nothing was exciting to her. She was determined to wear something different and attractive that night. She asked our other roommate, Amy, "Can I please look through your closet to see if I can find something to wear tonight?"

Amy paused for a moment before hesitantly answering, "Okay, but nothing is going to fit you. We wear different sizes." "I'll just check," Michelle said, and she walked straight into Amy's room and eagerly opened her closet door. I could see the look on Amy's face turn from patience to exasperation as she watched Michelle grab each hanger, pull it out to see the item in its entirety and then, after deciding it wasn't for her, forcefully push it back in place. At last Michelle found a multicolored top she liked. "Oh, I like this one," she said. "Can I try it on?" "I guess," Amy said with annoyance, "but it isn't going to fit you anyway." Not listening, Michelle pulled the top over her head, glanced in the mirror and happily exclaimed, "It fits me. I love it. It's perfect for tonight!" Hearing this, Amy immediately responded, "Can't you find something to wear in your own closet?" "No," Michelle said, "I'm tired of wearing the same things over and over again." "Well," said Amy, angry that Michelle still wasn't picking up on her hints, "I'm sorry, but I've changed my mind. You can't borrow that top." "Why not?" Michelle demanded. "Because," Amy uttered, "I really like that top and I don't want you to get it dirty." Michelle's mouth dropped. "What? So now you think I'm a slob? Don't you think I would clean it if by chance I happen to spill something on it?" Amy answered, "I don't know what you would do, but I don't want to lend you my top. Besides, this is not a matter of life and death. If you don't wear my top, you won't have to go to the party naked! You have tons of clothes in your closet. Just find something there." Disappointed and angry, Michelle responded, "Fine. But don't bother to ask me for a favor."

What happened here? Amy made a communication blunder when she initially agreed to lend Michelle her top even though she didn't want to. Foolishly, Amy figured that Michelle wouldn't find anything in her closet that she liked or that fit her. But Michelle found something she wanted to borrow and at that point Amy had to accept it or start an argument. Amy was too angry to let it go, so she changed her mind midstream and created a definite rift in their relationship.

COMMUNICATION BLUNDER

When someone you like asks you for a favor and you don't want to do it, it is a blunder to agree to do it.

In the next story you will again see how this communication blunder weakens a relationship. Then you will learn the communication wonder that gets you off the hook, reduces the tension of the moment and wins the respect of your friends. Jill and Leslie enjoy being friends. But on this very cold winter day, remaining friends proves to be a problem for both of them. It's Sunday afternoon and after sleeping late they are on the phone having a relaxing conversation about the week's events. Suddenly Leslie says, "Jill, I have to ask you a favor." Jill expects Leslie to ask her to do something simple, like reschedule their Thursday night dinner plans. But as Leslie continues talking, Jill realizes that Leslie's favor is not going to be that simple. Leslie says, "I was invited to an old college friend's wedding at the beginning of next month. I haven't seen a lot of my college friends in a while so I'd really like to go. But I have a small problem and here's where you can help me out. The wedding is in another state, so if I go, I have to buy a plane ticket, reserve a hotel room and buy a wedding gift. But right now my funds are a little tight." Jill's heart starts to beat faster. Jill thinks, "She isn't, she wouldn't, she couldn't be asking to borrow money to go to the wedding, could she?" Leslie continues, "So I was hoping you could lend me three hundred and fifty dollars, especially since you just mentioned that you got an unexpected tax refund last week. I'll pay you back in two months. Can you help me out?" Jill doesn't know what to say. It's true she does have some extra cash on hand but she doesn't like lending money because of a bad experience she had with an ex-friend who borrowed money from her and never paid her back. Jill also knows that although Lisa is a friend, she isn't one of her more reliable friends. Worried, Jill thinks, "If I do this favor for Leslie and she doesn't pay me back on time, I know it will ruin our friendship."

Jill tries to muster up the courage to say no, but she can't seem to do it because she knows that she'll have to give Leslie a reason and there is nothing truthful she could say that wouldn't end up insulting Leslie. So Jill says, "Are you sure you'll be able to pay me back in two months?" "Absolutely," Leslie immediately responds. "Okay, then I guess I'll lend you the money." "Thanks so much, Jill. You're a real lifesaver. Why don't I stop over tonight to pick up a check." "Tonight?" Jill asks. "Can't you wait until I see you for dinner on Thursday?" Leslie replies, "Well, I guess that will be okay." When Jill hangs up the phone she thinks that Leslie has a lot of nerve asking to borrow money for something that is so unnecessary. Jill is very upset that she agreed to lend Leslie the money, but she didn't see any other way out.

Jill made a communication blunder when she agreed to do her friend a favor that she didn't want to do. What Jill didn't know was the communication wonder about having a policy, which would have gotten her off the hook with dignity and self-respect. Jill should have confidently said, "Leslie, I'm sorry, but I have a policy about this. I don't lend money to friends." This way Jill could have said a polite no along with a supporting reason—"I have a policy about this." Although Leslie would not have liked Jill's answer, she would have accepted it without starting an argument because Jill had a reason for saying no—her policy. Giving a reason for your refusal softens your no response and gets you off the hook. In the long run, this communication wonder would also have worked to discourage Leslie from asking Jill to lend her money again, because Leslie would be aware of her policy of not lending money to friends.

COMMUNICATION WONDER

Get Off the Hook

When someone you like asks you for a favor that you don't want to do and you're concerned about hurting his or her feelings and creating a conflict, say, "I'm sorry, but I have a policy about this. I don't ____ [fill in the blank]."

Rule 20

· · · · · ·

Appreciate Criticism

PEOPLE HAVE DIFFERING OPINIONS. It's what makes us unique. But what makes my blood boil is when someone is so certain that their opinion is correct that they not only think it's acceptable to criticize another person's decision, they actually have the nerve to tell that person what to do. I call people who give uncalled-for criticism "know-it-alls." We encounter know-it-alls all the time. They may be our parents, our siblings, our colleagues or even friends who occasionally let their mouths run wild.

More than once while mediating legal disputes, the whole mediation process would come to a halt when one person gave uncalled-for criticism, the other person retaliated, and they quickly got into a heated argument. Defending oneself against uncalled-for criticism always creates stress and conflict. Trying to convince a know-it-all that he is wrong is like trying to swim against the current. I realized that being prepared with the right words to effectively handle uncalled-for criticism from a know-it-all is beneficial for everyone involved. In the following stories you will see what happens when people respond the wrong way to uncalled-for criticism and then you will learn the communication wonder that gives you the right words to gracefully end an argument before it begins.

Some years ago, before I discovered the words to quickly and gracefully end a hot encounter with a know-it-all, I was having a telephone conversation with one of my cousins. I usually enjoy talking to her, but every once in a while she forces her opinion on me and we end up in an argument. On this day, I casually said, "I can't talk for long because I have dinner plans with a friend and I have to stop at the ATM to get money before I meet her." She asked, "What's the big hurry? Why don't you just use your credit card for dinner?" "Well," I said, "the money isn't for me, it's for my friend Alyssa. I told her yesterday that I would lend her some money until she gets a new job."

My cousin then quickly jumped in to criticize my decision. "I know you should never lend money to a friend. You might not get your money back for a long time—or ever, for that matter. I never lend money to anyone and you shouldn't either." I was instantly annoyed at my cousin's uncalled-for criticism. It was my choice, not hers, to lend Alyssa money. My decision had absolutely nothing to do with her and she had no right to tell me what to do. So I defensively replied, "You don't know what you're talking about. Good friends lend each other money and I trust Alyssa. It's not your place to tell me what to do." My comment made her even more adamant about not lending friends money. She proclaimed, "Your friend isn't working now and if she doesn't find a job, she won't pay you back. You'll see. It's too bad but you're going to have to learn the hard way like I did."

The more my cousin tried to convince me that she was right, the harder I tried to convince her that she was wrong. We were both getting drawn into an argument even though it was clear from the onset that neither of us would give in and there really was no right or wrong thing to do anyway. At last, I said, "It's late, I have to go," to which my cousin's parting words were, "You better think about what I said." We ended the conversation irritated and resentful.

Although I blame my cousin for making a know-it-all comment that started the argument, the truth is, I was a full-fledged participant in the conflict. I couldn't control what she said, but I could control how I responded. The conversation turned into an argument because I got caught in the trap of arguing about whose position was right. I made a communication blunder when I responded to my cousin's opinion with defensive, retaliatory words. By choosing to counterattack, I actually persuaded her to become angrier and more certain of her opinion. The more each of us defended a position, the more heated our argument became.

Being defensive can quickly turn a peaceful conversation into an argument. When I was working as a mediator at a courthouse in Boston, I was asked to help two neighbors, Richard and Steve, resolve their conflict. They lived in a house that was divided into two co-op apartments. Richard owned and lived in the top floor and Steve owned and lived in the bottom floor. They shared a common driveway. We sat in a private room and I began the mediation session by asking Steve why he filed the lawsuit. Steve explained, "I filed this lawsuit because I own half of the driveway. Richard owns the other half, but six months ago his son moved in with him and since then his son has taken over the whole driveway for his car repair business. I used to park my car in the driveway, but now because of his son's business, I can barely get my car into the driveway and sometimes I even have to park on the street. I want him to stop using my side of the driveway, and I also want him to pay for his use of it for the last six months."

I asked him, "Have you talked to Richard about this?" "Yes, I've tried," he asserted, "but he seems to think it's no big deal and that he can do whatever he wants." I turned to Richard and asked him to tell us his side of the story.

"Well, I own half the driveway as well," Richard said. "My son lives with me now and he is entitled to use the driveway for his car repair business. Every time Steve came to talk to me about this situation he just yelled and told me that it's illegal for my son to run his business using the driveway. But Steve is wrong. It's legal. If Steve wasn't yelling about my son's business all the time, I might have understood that his real problem was not the business, but that Steve has trouble parking in the driveway. It always seemed to me that there was enough room for him to park his car. Look, I could make sure that my son's cars are moved out of the driveway by five o'clock before Steve gets home from work. We can leave the cars that are being repaired on the street overnight and also on the weekends."

With that said, I saw an easy opportunity for Richard and

Steve to settle the lawsuit. I asked, "Steve, what do you think about Richard's idea?" "Yes, I guess that would be okay," Steve answered. "I won't make you pay me rent for the last six months as long as you agree that from now on, you'll get the cars out of the driveway so I can park there." I was delighted that Richard and Steve were able to reach an agreement so quickly. I pulled out a blank settlement form to begin drafting a specific settlement agreement, but just then, Steve opened his mouth to say one more thing. "You know," he said, "we would never have had this problem if your thirty-five-year-old son hadn't moved back in with you. I know he's the problem. It's time you kicked him out."

I quickly looked at Richard and hoped he wouldn't take the bait, but he did. He ferociously responded, "Don't you tell me what to do. It's my house and I'll do whatever I want. You should be so lucky to have a son like mine." And that was it. Steve and Richard started fighting with one defensive comment followed by another. Even after I had calmed them down, they refused to sign the settlement paper they had agreed to sign just moments before. Now Steve didn't want cars on his side of the driveway at any time and he went back to demanding money for the use of the driveway for the past six months. Of course, Richard would not agree to this. The lawsuit couldn't be resolved in mediation, so Richard and Steve would have to come back to court another day to face the judge.

Steve made a mistake by being a know-it-all and making an uncalled-for comment about Richard's son. Richard made a communication blunder when he responded to Steve's criticism with his own defensive and retaliatory comments. Richard had the power to calm the situation down with the

right words that would have resulted in a desirable settlement, but instead he continued to fuel the argument with
his defensive words. Although you may not find yourself in a
court mediation setting, the principle illustrated in this story
applies to everyday situations—retaliating against someone who
is criticizing you incites the argument and makes the situation
worse.

COMMUNICATION BLUNDER

It is a blunder to become defensive and retaliate
against a person who criticizes you.

In this last story, you will see how Judy's defensive response
to her mother's uncalled-for criticism intensifies rather than
ends the argument. Then you will learn the communication
wonder for responding to uncalled-for criticism so you can
end an argument before it begins.

Judy, who stopped at the supermarket on her way home
from work, has just arrived at home. She greets her husband
and children, who are sitting in the den, and asks them to
help her carry the grocery bags from the car into the kitchen.
They help her out, but before she puts the food away, the
doorbell rings. She walks to the front door, opens it and
hears a melodic voice ask, "Hi, sweetheart, how are you?" It's
none other than her mother, Fran, and her father, Jack. "I'm
fine, Mom, but aren't you an hour early?" "Well," Fran says,
"we're just so excited to see Jon on his tenth birthday that we
couldn't wait to come over and give him his present." Unfor-

tunately, Judy is not as excited to have her parents arrive early. She hasn't even started to prepare the birthday dinner.

Judy tells her parents to join her husband and children in the den while she returns to the kitchen to put away the food and start dinner. However, Judy's mother follows her into the kitchen to see if she can help her with dinner. Fran looks around the kitchen and notices the frozen prepared meals on the counter. "You serve frozen packaged meals?" she asks with a disapproving look on her face. "You know, I never did that when you were young. I know it would be a lot healthier for your children if you made them home-cooked meals like I did for you and your brother. Maybe you should put in fewer hours at the office so you have more time to give your family what they deserve."

Judy can't believe her mother has the nerve to say this to her. She automatically responds, "Mom, I work hard all day so that I can give my kids everything they deserve. Just because they sometimes eat frozen dinners doesn't mean I'm a bad mother. Besides, I usually add fresh ingredients to the package anyway. Tonight I'm cooking dinner, so you can stop complaining." "I'm not talking about tonight. I'm talking about all the other times you're not there for your kids," her mother responds. Judy, very agitated now, says, "You know something, I don't remember you winning the Mother of the Year Award!" "What do you mean by that?" her mother snaps back. "I was a great mother. I always cooked. I was always home for you and your brother. With your schedule, you don't even see your kids until dinnertime and sometimes you don't get home until after dinner. How can you compare us?" Now Judy is hooked into the argument and she adds more fuel to the fire by saying, "You know, Mom, times have changed. You're just so old-fashioned. What you say doesn't make sense anymore. I'm sick of listening to you tell me what to do with my family. You should mind your own business."

As soon as the words leave Judy's mouth, she realizes she should not have said them. It's her son's birthday and the argument with her mother has changed the tone of the evening.

Judy is upset with herself for allowing the argument to go from a simmer to a boil. She made a communication blunder when she responded to her mother's critical comments by counterattacking and raising the level of friction between them. Judy knows she needs a better way to handle situations like this because her mother will never change. If their arguments are going to end, it's going to be up to Judy to change her responses to her mother's inciting words.

What could Judy have done to cleverly put out the sparks of this familiar argument before it began? Judy should have let go of trying to change her mother's mind. Instead, she should have saved her energy and reduced her stress by focusing the conversation on appreciating her mother's criticism rather than fighting it. Sound crazy? No, not at all. Appreciating criticism doesn't mean that Judy agrees with her mother; it simply means that Judy should let her mother know that she heard her opinion and will consider it.

Judy should have used this communication wonder to calmly say to her mother in a respectful tone, "Mom, thank you for giving me your opinion. I will definitely give it some thought." Then Judy should have changed the subject. In that way, Judy would have shown her mother that she heard what she said and she would consider her opinion. If her mother had continued to be critical, Judy should have repeated the communication wonder. It may seem bizarre to appreciate criticism when you disagree with it, but at the end of the day, when you know you can't change someone's mind, it is the best way to respond. When you appreciate criticism you surprise the other person with your nonaggressive response and you instantly change the direction of the conversation and reduce the tension. Using this communication wonder would have gotten Judy the result she wanted—a peaceful resolution to uncalled-for criticism—and her mother would have gotten the result she wanted—the feeling that Judy was listening to her. It would have ended this disagreement without forcing Judy or her mother to admit that she was wrong.

The key is to make this communication wonder your automatic response when you receive uncalled-for criticism. Don't get defensive with a friend, a family member or a colleague when he or she gives you uncalled-for criticism. Instead, be smart—become appreciative.

COMMUNICATION WONDER

Appreciate Criticism

When someone gives you uncalled-for criticism, say, "Thank you for giving me your opinion. I will definitely give it some thought."

Rule 21

· · · · ·

Get a Green Light

DO YOU EVER GET the sense that you're talking to someone but he isn't hearing a word you're saying? Can you think of a time when you were convinced that a friend, family member or colleague didn't understand what you said because he was distracted by something else even though he seemed to be listening to you? I'm going to show you an easy way to make sure that people give you their full attention when you talk.

When I was at law school I called a friend at her law firm because I was considering applying for a job at her firm and I wanted to get some information from her. I spent five minutes telling her what kind of law I wanted to practice and the kind of work environment I preferred. I assumed my friend was listening to me because she would occasionally respond with "uh-huh" or "okay." When I finished talking, I asked her, "So, do you think your firm has what I'm looking for?" She hesitantly responded, "Um, what exactly did you say you're looking for?" With that response I realized that she hadn't heard anything I said. Although I was annoyed, I started to repeat what I had already told her. She suddenly interrupted me and said, "Laurie, I have a meeting in five minutes and I'm in the middle of finishing a memo for the meeting. Can I call you back later?" "Yes, you can call me back later," I muttered in response, and we hung up. I quickly realized that the reason she hadn't been listening to me was because she was busy working on her memo while we were on the phone. I was annoyed with her for not giving me her full attention, for wasting my time and for abruptly ending the conversation. I wasn't interested in talking to her again later.

This type of irritating exchange happens all the time. People often let other people talk to them even though they are barely listening. Wouldn't it be easier if we could find out before we begin talking, whether or not the person is ready, willing and able to listen? The answer is yes. I have created a communication wonder that quickly tells you whether you have a green light to begin talking to someone with his full attention, or a red light, which means you should remain silent because the person will be inattentive and distracted. In the following stories I will show you the effects of picking the wrong time to talk to someone and then I will share my simple communication wonder that helps you determine the right time to talk to get someone's full attention.

All relationships, no matter how good they are, suffer from occasional misunderstandings and conflicts. One Sunday afternoon Donald was watching television in the den. He flipped channels for a while until he came across a spy thriller movie. The movie had just started and he had not seen it so he decided to watch it. After being glued to the TV for almost an hour, his wife, Elaine, nonchalantly came into the den. She walked over to the couch where Donald was sitting and said, "Donald, your mother just called and asked us to have dinner with her next weekend. She wants me to call her back today to let her know whether Friday or Saturday night is better for us and what kind of food we want to eat. So which night do you prefer and what do you want to eat?" Donald, his eyes darting between the television and his wife, trying to listen to both, quickly responded, "Yes, sure." Elaine, annoyed by his answer because it had nothing to do with her question, took a step closer to him and asked, "Donald, are you listening to me? I asked you whether you want to have dinner with your mother on Friday or Saturday night and what kind of food you want." "Uh, I don't know," he said, staring at the television. "Either day is fine." Elaine, really annoyed now, said even louder, "You're not listening to me. I don't know why I bothered to ask you."

Now that got Donald's attention. "Elaine," he said, finally turning his body to focus his eyes on her, "I've been watching this movie for an hour and I like it. Can't you just wait? We don't have to decide about dinner right now." Elaine, clearly irritated, responded, "Well, how was I supposed to know you were so intent on watching this movie? Why didn't you tell me? I heard you flipping channels before so I thought you were just randomly watching something on TV. Go ahead and watch the stupid movie!"

What happened here? Elaine made a communication blunder when she assumed that Donald was ready to give her his full attention. She didn't realize that he was paying attention to a movie when she asked him an important question. As a result, when he didn't give her his full attention, Elaine felt ignored and became annoyed with him. Then Donald became annoyed with her for expecting him to stop doing what he was doing to talk to her. Does this situation sound familiar? Clearly, picking the wrong time to talk to someone is a sure way to persuade that person not to listen to you.

This communication blunder commonly occurs when two people are on the phone. For example, see what happens when Cheryl calls her friend Martha, who is already on the phone with someone else. Martha hears the call waiting signal so she asks the person she's talking to to hold on while she picks up the second call. "Hello," Martha says. Cheryl replies, "Hi, Martha, it's Cheryl." Cheryl assumes this is a good time to talk to Martha because she answered the phone, so she immediately begins, "I'm so glad you're home. I just got back from my vacation in Vermont. The trip was fantastic!" Martha replies, "That's nice." She wants to tell Cheryl that she needs to call her back because she is on the line with someone else, but Cheryl doesn't give her the chance. Instead Cheryl quickly says, "The kids went skiing for the first time and loved it." "Oh," Martha says, and again before she can say that she's on the phone Cheryl starts to describe their hotel. When Cheryl is in the middle of a sentence, Martha has no choice but to interrupt her. "Cheryl, I have to go. I have someone waiting on the other line." "Oh, really?" Cheryl responds, her enthusiasm now dulled. "I didn't know you were on another call. Why didn't you tell me before I went into the whole story about my vacation?" Martha replies, "Well, you started to tell me about your vacation the second I said hello so I didn't have a chance. Anyway, I really don't have the time to talk right now. I'll call you back later." "Fine," Cheryl says, annoyed with her friend for rudely cutting her off.

Cheryl hangs up and is insulted because Martha cut her off in the middle of her story about her ski trip. But it wasn't Martha who caused this strife, it was Cheryl. Cheryl made a communication blunder when she assumed that because Martha answered the phone, she was ready, willing and able to give Cheryl her full attention.

COMMUNICATION BLUNDER

It is a blunder to assume that someone is ready to give you his full attention whenever you have something important to say.

In the next story you will observe another situation in which someone picks the wrong time to talk. Tom, who has been working in Customer Service at a phone company for a few months, decides to tell his boss about a clever idea that he has to speed up the customer complaint response time. So after lunch, Tom, aware that his boss encourages his employees to stop by his office, knocks on his door. "Yes? Come right in," says Mr. Strauss, his boss, who is sitting at his desk writing something. Tom opens the door, walks into his office and sits down in the chair in front of Mr. Strauss's desk. Tom begins to speak. "Mr. Strauss, I wanted to see you to discuss a new plan I have to speed up the customer complaint response time." Mr. Strauss nods his head and says, "Okay," but looks up at Tom for only a moment before continuing to write and focus on the papers on his desk. Tom knows that Mr. Strauss is being rude by not looking at him while he's talking, but Tom continues anyway, oblivious that Mr. Strauss is concentrating on an important status report. After a few uh-huhs and swift glances from his boss, Tom finishes talking and hopes that his boss is interested in his plan. Tom asks, "What do you think of my idea?" Mr. Strauss puts down his pen, looks directly at Tom and says, "Your idea? Tom, I'm not clear on what you're proposing. Besides, this is not the right time to change anything at the company. Let's talk about this another time. Thanks for stopping by." With that, Tom says, "Okay," and sarcastically adds, "and thanks for listening to me." He stands up and walks out of the office believing that Mr. Strauss is rude and closed-minded.

But Tom is quite wrong about that. What happened here was that Tom simply picked the wrong time to talk to his boss. Tom made a communication blunder when he assumed that because his boss invited him in, this was a green light to begin talking about his idea. Tom was so caught up in what he wanted to say that he didn't realize Mr. Strauss was busy working on something else. And Mr. Strauss, like many people, thought he could do two things at once so he didn't tell Tom that he was busy and that this was not a good time to talk. As a result, Tom walked out of his boss's office feeling ignored, unappreciated and resentful.

How could Tom have known that his boss was not ready to give him his full attention? He needed to use a communication wonder. When Tom walked into his boss's office the first thing he should have said was, "Mr. Strauss, I want to talk to you about something important. Is this a good time for you?"

That question—"Is this a good time for you?"—is a communication wonder, because it would have let Mr. Strauss know that Tom wanted his full attention, and it would have encouraged Mr. Strauss to tell Tom that he was involved in something and it was not a good time for him. Then Tom and Mr. Strauss could have selected a better time to meet.

This communication wonder would have helped Tom avoid the friction and irritation that develops between two people when one person wants to talk and the other person isn't ready to listen. Don't expect that when someone says hello on the phone or "Come in" that he wants to hear what you have to say. Use the communication wonder to ask the important question "Is this a good time for you?" If you get a red light, a no answer, stop talking and arrange a better time to talk to that person. But if you get a welcome green light, a yes answer, start talking and go for it!

COMMUNICATION WONDER

Get a Green Light

Before you delve into an important conversation with someone, ask, "Is this a good time for you?"

Rule 22

. . . . .

Rein in Roaming Anger

YOU KNOW IT'S BAD when your friend calls you at work just to tell you how angry she is with another friend of hers. Then, that evening, she calls you at home to tell you the same thing. You have lunch with her over the weekend and she's still talking about how mad she is at that other person for what she did. Finally, you can't take it anymore. "If you're so angry," you exclaim, "please tell her, not me!" "Who me? Angry? I'm not angry. This whole thing is really no big deal," responds your friend. "Well, you could have fooled me," you say and quickly change the subject.

We've all been around people who desperately try to suppress their anger and pretend that they are indifferent to a situation. More than likely, each of us can recall a time when we were angry with someone and chose not to tell that person how we felt. We hoped that eventually our anger would disappear and the relationship would return to normal.

Unfortunately, suppressed anger often becomes like trash in the garbage. If no one takes out the garbage at the end of the day, it's tolerable. But if several days go by and the garbage builds up, it begins to smell. In fact, the smell might even spread into other rooms. The same can be said about the suppression of anger. If we do not let it out, at first it might seem that we have avoided a conflict, but over time our anger builds and the relationship suffers from bitterness and resentment. Our anger begins to roam to the people around us.

If we want to keep our relationships healthy, we must acknowledge that there is a time when we must speak our mind and go directly to the source of our anger. We may choose to confront a problem early on, but if we choose not to, we need to be aware of the danger of roaming anger. In the stories below you will see how suppressing anger can affect relationships. Then you will learn the communication wonder that tells you when you have no other choice but to confront the source of your anger.

Phyllis and Harvey are married. Phyllis is a sixth-grade elementary school science teacher. One Wednesday evening when her husband walked in the door from work, Phyllis began telling him about how angry she was with Anne, her good friend who also worked at the elementary school. "Harvey," she said, "do you remember that today was the monthly teachers' meeting?" "Yes," Harvey affirmed. "Did you present your idea for a school play?" "Yes," Phyllis replied, "but my idea was almost rejected because of something my supposed good friend

Anne said at the meeting. I'm so angry with her." "What did she say?" Harvey asked, curious. "Well, after I presented my idea for a school play and I volunteered to direct it everyone seemed to like my idea, and I felt really good. That is, until Anne opened her big mouth and announced, 'I don't think we should consider putting on a play since none of us, including Phyllis, has any dramatic experience. I don't want the students to take part in a play that's not run by a professional. We should hire a qualified drama teacher to direct it so that it turns out right.' Then the whole discussion turned to the expense of hiring a drama teacher and everyone turned against the idea. Then I spoke up and explained that the purpose of the play was not to produce a Broadway show but to expose the students to acting and encourage them to work together toward a common goal. I explained that I was fully confident that I could handle directing a play. After that, the discussion shifted to a more positive note. Although Anne voted against the play, it was approved by the majority. I'm happy that the teachers agreed with me and saw the value of putting on a play, but I'm so hurt and angry with Anne for what she said to publicly make me look incompetent. Until today, I considered her one of my closest friends at school."

"I can't say I'm surprised," Harvey responded. "Haven't you noticed that Anne has a tendency to say the wrong thing at the wrong time? What did you say to her after the meeting?" "I didn't say anything. Why would I? There was no way she could take back her words and I didn't want to risk getting into an argument with her. I decided to let it ride. Okay, enough about me, let's talk about you. How was your day?" Their conversation continued and Phyllis didn't mention the Anne fiasco again, at least not that night.

The next day when Harvey and Phyllis were in the kitchen preparing dinner, Harvey asked, "What play are you going to do?" "I don't know yet. I haven't given it a lot of thought. Every time I think about the play I get sidetracked thinking about what Anne said about me at the meeting yesterday." Harvey asked, "Did you have lunch with her today as usual?" "Yes, but other people sat with us, so I acted like everything was fine. I hoped she would apologize, but she said nothing about the incident all day. She acted like nothing was wrong! It seems to me that she doesn't even realize that she insulted me. I think I'll avoid eating with her tomorrow."

Harvey could see that his wife was still upset by the situation so he suggested, "Don't you think you should talk to Anne about what happened at the meeting? Maybe she's unaware that what she said hurt you. You should give her the chance to apologize." "No, I don't want to deal with it. Besides, the teachers approved the play in spite of her critical comments about me." "Okay, if you think that's best," responded Harvey. "I do," Phyllis said as she placed the salad bowl on the table.

Two days later, on Friday, Phyllis and Harvey went out to dinner. Harvey didn't ask Phyllis about school because he was afraid that it would lead to another tirade against Anne. He understood that Phyllis was upset with her friend, but listening to her complain about Anne was annoying. But Harvey couldn't fend off that undesirable subject for long. "I saw Anne at lunch today," Phyllis began. "Uh-huh," Harvey responded. "But I didn't sit with her. I think she noticed." "Uh-huh," Harvey said, not wanting to encourage the conversation. Phyllis continued, "I think she might recognize my coldness and realize that she said something wrong. Do you think that will happen?" Harvey responded sharply, "How should I know?"

Phyllis didn't like his tone and asked, "Why are you getting annoyed with me? I'm mad at Anne, not you." Harvey replied, "Yes, I understand. I'd be mad at her too, but this is the third time this week that you've brought up Anne and I've had enough of it. If someone I cared about upset me like that I'd go right to that person and speak my mind instead of telling you about it over and over again. So stop saying there's no point in talking to her about it. Just go and talk to her. If you won't do it for the sake of your friendship, do it for me!" "Well, Harvey, now that you've said that, you don't have to worry anymore. I won't mention Anne, the play or school to you ever again because you obviously don't care." "Fine!" Harvey responded. What had been a pleasant dinner conversation quickly turned into an argument.

Phyllis made a communication blunder when she let her anger roam straight to Harvey by repeatedly telling him how angry she was with Anne instead of telling Anne herself. By suppressing her anger, her negative feelings toward Anne did not decrease over time, they increased. Phyllis's roaming anger caused her to avoid Anne at work and created a problem between herself and her husband.

COMMUNICATION BLUNDER

It is a blunder to repeatedly tell one person about a problem you have with another person.

In the next story, you will see how my friend Tracy involved me in a conflict she had with Heather, another friend of ours. One Saturday night, Heather invited me, Tracy, Brian, a coworker, and about a dozen other people to a party in her apartment. From the moment Tracy and Brian met that night, they clicked.

They began dating and about a month later when I met Tracy for dinner, she told me that she was seeing Brian exclusively. "That's great," I said. "Does Heather know you two are still dating?" "Oh," Tracy said, "I don't want to talk about Heather," but then surprisingly she went right on to talk about her. "Now that Brian and I have been going out steadily, Brian told me something Heather said about me that I don't like. It seems that a week ago Brian overheard Heather talking about me with some of her other friends at work. She said, 'I have a friend Tracy who can't be trusted with men. She dates a few men at once, conveniently strings them along and then dumps them.' She actually said that I can't be trusted! I'm so angry with her." "But Brian knows that what she said isn't true, right?" "Of course. Brian and I are getting along great and he trusts me completely. I think Heather may be jealous because of all the dates I've had. Maybe she would be happier if I stayed home and became an old maid." "Possibly," I replied, quite surprised at what Tracy had just revealed.

"So, have you talked to Heather about this?" I asked. "No. Brian thinks I should, but I decided against it. I'll just be more careful from now on about what I tell her about my personal life. Obviously, Heather's the one who can't be trusted, not me." "Well," I said, attempting to mediate the situation, "if that's how you see it. But you might consider the possibility that Heather could have been joking or that Brian misinterpreted what she said." "Hey, saying that I can't be trusted isn't a joke to me." "Tracy, I know that you and Heather have been friends for a long time; you should talk to her and try to work this out." "I could, but I'm not in the mood to start up with her. I'm just going to let it slide." Tracy dropped the subject and went on to talk about a movie she had seen recently.

A week later, I had dinner with Tracy, Brian and a couple of other friends. I found out ahead of time that someone had invited Heather and she was joining us. As I approached the restaurant, I remembered my conversation with Tracy the week before and I hoped for everyone's sake that she had resolved her problem with Heather. Throughout dinner I noticed that Tracy avoided talking directly to Heather. Tracy was apparently still angry with her, and from my observations, I didn't think Heather had a clue.

At the end of the meal Tracy and I excused ourselves to go to the restroom. Tracy checked to be sure there was no one else in there. Then she said, "Can you believe her? Acting all sweet and nice like that?" I understood Tracy's anger, but I felt compelled to say, "Tracy, I see that the problem with Heather is still bothering you, but you have to realize that she doesn't know what you're thinking because you didn't tell her. She might not remember what she said to her friends in the office." "I don't care what she remembers. Right now I don't want to be around her. Brian and I are not going out to the club with the rest of you after dinner. We'll do our own thing." There was nothing I could say to change her mind. We returned to the table and paid the bill. Everyone left the restaurant. Tracy and Brian went one way and the rest of us went another.

The next day I called Tracy. We chatted about dinner and then she started up again. Tracy began talking about Heather's inexcusable behavior toward her. I couldn't listen to her any-

more so I said, "Tracy, this is the third time you've brought
this up. The problem you have with Heather will not go away
by talking to me." "Laurie, I've already told you that I'm not
going to talk to Heather about this. If you don't want to talk
about this with me, then don't talk to me."

Tracy didn't realize that by trying to suppress her anger, she
was making the situation worse. What could have been a single, short, uncomfortable conversation with Heather had turned
into deep resentment, and Tracy's roaming anger was landing
on me. As I saw it, if Tracy didn't deal directly with Heather
soon and give her the opportunity to explain her version of
what happened, all of our friendships would suffer perma-
nently.

Even though it was Heather who made the initial mistake
by talking about Tracy behind her back, Tracy was equally
responsible because she handled the situation poorly. Tracy
couldn't control Heather's actions or words, but she could
control the way she responded to them. Tracy should have
used a communication wonder to recognize that there was a
definite time to stop complaining to me and go directly to
Heather, the source of her anger. Although going to Heather
would have risked conflict, getting things out in the open would
have dissipated Tracy's growing animosity and eliminated her
roaming anger. Tracy should have known that it was time to go
to the source of her anger when she complained to me about
Heather for the *third* time.

In any relationship, there are times during which people
hurt each other and get angry. The key to this communication
wonder is to pay attention to those times. If you don't deal effectively with your anger immediately, then you should check
to see if you are repeatedly complaining about your problem

to someone else. If you are, then that is your cue. It is time to go to the source of your anger. It's time to give that person the opportunity to recognize, explain or deny what he or she said or did. When someone is important to you and you want your relationship with them to succeed, be sure to go to the source to eliminate your roaming anger.

COMMUNICATION WONDER

Rein in Roaming Anger

If you're angry with someone and you don't tell him, but you do tell someone else about it on three separate occasions, it's time to confront the person who made you angry.

Rule 23

· · · · ·

Avoid Empty Gestures

CAN YOU THINK OF a time when someone surprised you by offering to help you out, then didn't follow through on the offer? Maybe that person offered to help you move, to host a birthday party for you or even to put you in touch with someone who could help you get a job or a new client. At first you appreciated his kindness, but as time passed and he never brought up the subject again, that appreciation wore off and turned into mistrust and resentment. You wondered, "Did he forget about the offer? Was it an empty gesture? Did he change his mind? Should I mention it to him again?" Truthfully, people make offers all the time on the spur of the moment and then don't follow through on them once the moment is

past. I call these "empty offers" because they have no sub-
stance. Unfortunately, they create more stress and disappointment in a relationship than one might expect.

A person who makes an empty offer doesn't usually have
malicious intentions. In fact, it's just the opposite. He makes
the offer because he wants to please people. The problem is
that when he makes the offer on the spur of the moment, he
tends to say it without thinking it through. When the conversation is over, so is his offer. But the person who receives the
offer remembers it because it is important to him and he eagerly looks forward to the follow-through.

I'll bet that while you *can* recall many times when someone
made an empty offer to you, you probably *cannot* recall any
times that you gave an empty offer to someone. All of us need
to become aware of how easy it is to open our mouth to make
an empty gesture that ends up disturbing the very person we
are trying to please. Read the following stories to learn how to
prevent yourself from making an empty offer that persuades
someone to dislike and mistrust you.

One morning Denise told her department head, Kim, that
she wouldn't be able to attend the weekly status meeting that
afternoon because she had to leave work early to be home for
a 5 P.M. furniture delivery. "What are you having delivered?"
Kim asked. "I'm getting a new bedroom set and a desk." "Are
you buying any other furniture?" "Yes, I'm planning to buy a
dining table and chairs and a convertible couch for the living
room. It's just too expensive to buy everything at once. Next
week I'm going to start shopping around for the best deals."
"Wait a minute, I think I can help you out," Kim quickly replied.
"One of my neighbors owns a fantastic furniture store in the
city. He has a great selection of convertible couches at low

prices. I bought mine there. I'm sure if I ask him, he'd give you a sizable discount." "Wow!" Denise said. "That would be great." "No problem," Kim replied. "I'll talk to my neighbor about the discount and get back to you." "Thank you so much."

Throughout the next two weeks, every time Denise saw Kim at work she remembered their conversation about the furniture discount and hoped Kim would volunteer to give her the information she had offered. But Kim never said a word about the furniture. At first Denise made excuses to herself for Kim's delay. But as the days passed, Denise became more and more bothered by the whole experience of waiting for Kim to get back to her with the information. So one day at the end of the weekly status meeting, Denise caught up with Kim at the elevator. As they stood waiting, alone, Denise hoped that Kim would finally give her the furniture information she had offered. But Kim said nothing about it. Instead, she talked about the meeting they had just attended. Denise felt very uncomfortable reminding Kim of her offer because she was her department head. However, Denise was itching to buy a couch for her living room. So with some hesitation, Denise seized the moment and said, "Kim, remember when you offered to talk to your neighbor about getting me a discount at his furniture store? Well, I'm ready to buy the furniture now. What should I do?" "Oh," she responded. "I thought about it after I told you I would talk to my neighbor, and the truth is, I don't know him well enough to ask him for a favor for a friend. Sorry about that." Denise was struck by Kim's comment. She had waited patiently and not shopped around for furniture for weeks expecting to hear that Denise's neighbor would give her a good discount. Denise wondered, "How could Kim have made that offer with no intention of following through on it? How could she leave me hanging without getting back to me to tell me that she had decided not to talk to her neighbor?" Denise was upset and disappointed with Kim for acting so nonchalant about something that was so important to her.

Kim made a communication blunder when she made a spontaneous offer without following through on it. Why did she make this empty gesture in the first place? She was simply trying to please Denise and persuade her that she was a kind, helpful person. At first, her offer did persuade Denise to like and appreciate her because Denise was excited about getting a discount. But after Kim didn't get back to Denise about the offer, Denise began to think that Kim was rude and unreliable. Finally, when Kim told her that she had no intention of following through on her offer, Denise became extremely upset and disappointed in Kim. Kim shouldn't have made the offer in the first place, but at the very least, she should have gotten back to Denise to tell her that she wasn't going to follow through on it.

COMMUNICATION BLUNDER

Making an offer and not following
through on it is a blunder.

In the next story, you will see how another empty offer made in passing weakened a friendship. Mary and Rachel had been friends for many years and both of them had recently become friendly with Cathy, who started working in their office six months earlier. It was the very beginning of December when Mary, Rachel and Cathy were eating lunch together and the subject of New Year's Eve came up. "Cathy, what are you doing for New Year's Eve?" Mary asked. "I don't know," Cathy responded, "I haven't given it much thought. What about you, Mary?" "I don't have any plans," Mary answered. "Me neither," Rachel said, "although I was going to talk to some of my friends about New Year's Eve this week."

Cathy was eager to become better friends with Mary and Rachel so she spontaneously said, "You know what? Why don't I throw a New Year's Eve party in my apartment? I'll invite a lot of fun people from my old job. It would be nice to see them. Would you both come?" "Sure, count me in," Mary said. "That would be awesome," Rachel added. "I'd be happy to help you set up for the party." "Thanks," Cathy said. "New Year's will be great." With their plans settled, Mary and Rachel went back to work excited about Cathy's upcoming party.

Two weeks later Cathy was having second thoughts about throwing a New Year's party. She went over to Rachel's desk to explain the situation. "Rachel, remember how I said I would have a New Year's party? Well, I can't do it. I'm so busy that I don't have time to organize it. Besides, now that I think about it, my apartment is too small to accommodate a big party anyway." The look on Rachel's face revealed her disappointment. Cathy, aware that she was letting her friend down, quickly added, "Well, why don't you and Mary come over to my apartment to celebrate New Year's anyway? I'll cook something special for dinner, buy some great desserts and rent a movie. It'll be just the three of us. Okay?" This new offer didn't make Rachel any less annoyed with Cathy for revoking her original offer. Rachel had no desire to sit in front of the TV on New

Year's Eve with her two friends. She wanted to go to a party. But now, how could she bail out on Cathy and her dinner for three without hurting and offending her? Cornered, Rachel was forced to accept. "Okay, the three of us can all just hang out at your apartment." Rachel's New Year's Eve plans were ruined and she blamed Cathy. Rachel would never rely on Cathy again, for anything.

What happened here? Cathy blundered big time. Her effort to please her friends with her New Year's Eve offer fell flat on its face because she opened her mouth to make an offer before fully thinking through the details. Cathy assumed that everything would be fine after she explained to Rachel why she couldn't host a party. But things weren't fine because Rachel had been counting on her original offer. In the end, Cathy's empty gesture antagonized Rachel. In all likelihood, the empty offer would also annoy Mary once she found out about it. Ironically, Cathy's attempt to become closer to her two new friends only pushed them away.

How could Cathy have prevented this situation from occurring? Cathy should have known that people rely on offers made to them. Before making the offer Cathy should have asked herself, "Am I certain that I can follow through on hosting a New Year's Eve party?" She should have held her tongue while she thought ahead to the party, considering all the work involved, as well as the size of her apartment. If Cathy had given her offer some forethought, she wouldn't have made it in the first place or had to renege on it.

The important thing for all of us to learn is that you must take the time to think through an offer before you make it. Always assume that the person you make an offer to will take it seriously, even if you don't. There is no harm in withholding an offer for a day or more as you figure out whether or not you will be able to follow through on it. If you stop yourself from making an empty offer, even when your intentions are sincere and honorable, you will avoid disappointing and upsetting your friends, family members and colleagues. Use this simple communication wonder to maintain the trust and confidence of the people in your life.

COMMUNICATION WONDER

Avoid Empty Gestures

Before you make an offer, ask yourself, "Am I certain that I can follow through on it?" Wait to make the offer until you are certain that you can follow through.

Rule 24

· · · · ·

Create Comfort in a Difficult Time

IF SOMEONE IS SERIOUSLY ill or has experienced the death of someone close to him or her, you know there is nothing you can say or do that would change the situation. You feel sad and helpless, aware that you can't cure the illness or give life back to someone to make things better. You want to call the person at that time to say something comforting and sympathetic, but words fail you. You ask yourself, "What can I say that hasn't already been said many times before by others?" You anticipate and fear that awkward and unsettling moment at the start of your next conversation when you hear that person's voice. So what do you do? You avoid that stressful conversation.

But is avoidance the best thing to do? As you read the following stories, you will quickly discover that saying nothing sends the unintended message "I don't care about you." Unfortunately, that is generally the opposite of what you feel. When someone you care about is suffering, you have two choices. You can avoid the situation, say nothing and create distance and hurt feelings in your relationship, or you can see the situation as an opportunity to strengthen your relationship with that person and say something that is compassionate and caring. It is important to take action and reach out to others. You need to learn what to say when you don't know what to say to a friend, family member or colleague to help you cope with the temporary discomfort of a difficult conversation. The words you choose to say can also help the person move forward to enjoy the comfort of a better time.

My mother's friend Sharon told me about the circumstances that surrounded her illness. One day Sharon felt a sudden, slight tremor in her right arm. A doctor's visit led her to believe that she might be in an early stage of Parkinson's disease. Sharon said that during the weeks that followed she saw many doctors who did lots of medical tests to determine what was wrong. She was so exhausted that she had no interest in talking to any of her friends about what was going on in her life. In fact, she admitted to me later that her suspected physical illness created such anxiety and fear in her that she became so depressed she didn't want to go outside. She stopped going to church with her husband in spite of the fact that it was the highlight of her week. Fortunately, her husband was very understanding and helped her in every way he could.

Then one Sunday morning, a few weeks after the doctors confirmed that Sharon had Parkinson's disease, she came to a big decision. It was time for her to let her pastor and her church friends know the truth about her illness. It was a Sunday tradition at their church for the pastor to list the names of the congregates who were sick and ask everyone to pray for them. So just before her husband left for church that day Sharon said, "I want you to tell the pastor that I have Parkinson's disease and that's why I haven't been to church. Please let him know that I'll be back just as soon as I get the side effects of my medication under control." "Okay," her husband said. "I'll let the pastor know." "Oh, and there's one more thing," Sharon said. "Please check to see if Gladys is in church today. I want to be sure she knows why I've missed church and choir practice. I should have called her myself, but I've been so tired I just haven't had the energy to call anyone." Sharon's husband readily agreed to her requests. He hugged her and left for church.

During the next week, Sharon received phone calls from members of the congregation who wanted to wish her well after hearing the pastor's announcement that she had Parkinson's disease. Sharon appreciated each and every call she received. It made her feel good to know that people were thinking about her and cared about her. But she was disappointed that not one of the calls was from Gladys, her closest friend at church. Sharon asked her husband, "Honey, are you sure you saw Gladys at church last weekend?" "Yes, I'm sure. She was sitting two rows in front of me. Didn't she call you?" "No, she hasn't called. I'm really hurt by that," Sharon revealed. "I thought she would have called me as soon as she found out that I was ill." "Well, she should have called you," Sharon's husband said, "but, you know, sometimes people just don't know what to say in difficult situations like this. Anyway, it's not like she's your best friend. You only spend time with her at church and at choir practice."

Sharon didn't see it that way at all. "It doesn't matter how much time we spend together, I still feel close to her. If she was thinking about me and I mattered to her, she would have called. I would have called her if the situation was reversed." Sharon's husband didn't know how to respond. He couldn't understand why Gladys hadn't called either.

Why didn't Gladys call? Gladys didn't call because, as Sharon found out later from another friend, she just didn't know what to say. Gladys never considered the idea that she would insult Sharon by not calling her. You see, Gladys actually did care about Sharon but she saw the situation in an entirely different light. She feared she would make things worse for Sharon if she said the wrong thing at the wrong time. She worried about upsetting Sharon by bringing up the subject of Parkinson's disease. Basically, Gladys allowed her own anxieties to interfere with calling her friend. Gladys hoped that with time, things would improve and she would see Sharon in church. What Gladys didn't understand was that having that difficult conversation with Sharon at that time would have been much better than not having a conversation at all. Gladys made a serious communication blunder that persuaded Sharon to lose faith and confidence in their friendship.

COMMUNICATION BLUNDER

When someone you care about is ill or mourning the loss of someone close to him, it is a blunder to avoid calling that person.

In the next story you will see how important it is to overcome your fears and doubts about calling someone when he or she experiences a tragedy. Michael was at home one Saturday morning when he received a telephone call from the nurse who took care of his elderly mother, informing him that she had had another sudden, severe heart attack and died earlier that morning. Michael's mother had a serious heart condition and had been on medication since a major heart attack two years before. Michael was, of course, devastated by the news. Fortunately his wife, Rhonda, was home to console him. After a while he started to talk about the funeral but became too upset to continue the conversation. Rhonda told him, "I'll take care of all the arrangements and I'll call everyone to let them know about it." The next day, after Rhonda had arranged the funeral, she called some of their friends and relatives to give them the information. One of the people Rhonda called was Michael's good friend Sam.

About a week after the funeral Sam was talking to Richard, another friend of Michael's, and he told him about Michael's mother. "That's awful," Richard said. "I know that he was an only child and he was very close to his mother. How did you find out that she died?" "Rhonda called me and I went to the funeral," Sam said. "Oh," Richard said, wondering why neither Michael nor Rhonda had called him. "How's Michael doing?" "He's doing a little better now. He's still very upset, but he knows that his mother lived a long life. The other day he told me he's comforted by knowing that he was a good son and that his mother often told him so." When Sam and Richard's conversation ended, Richard walked away thinking, "I should probably call Michael and offer my condolences, but what should I say? I always feel such pressure calling someone at a time like this. It's so awkward." Trying to convince himself that it wasn't necessary to call Michael, Richard continued talking to himself. "I'll bet Michael's been getting a lot of phone calls from other people. Maybe he's had enough calls and doesn't want to keep on talking about his mother. He didn't call me, so maybe I don't have to call him." At last, Richard convinced himself that it would be okay if he didn't call Michael. He decided he'd wait to say something to Michael in person when he saw him again.

Meanwhile, Michael was slowly recovering from the loss of his mother. During the weeks after his mother's death he received many telephone calls from people offering their condolences and asking him if there was anything they could do to help. The fact was, Michael did need help from his friends. He needed help with the overwhelming task of emptying out his mother's house and getting rid of her furniture and belongings. Each telephone call he received made him feel a little better and reinforced his relationship with the person calling. Michael would never forget which friends took the time to call to find out how he was feeling and offer their help. Of course, Richard was not in the group of friends Michael would fondly remember as being there for him during that difficult time, because Richard never called him.

What happened here? Richard made a blunder when he made excuses to himself for not calling Michael to offer his condolences. In times of tragedy, who calls who first is meaningless, but what is meaningful is that a call is made to foster communication between the two people. Richard let his own anxieties get in the way of doing the right thing. He underestimated the significance of a phone call to Michael and overlooked an important opportunity to persuade Michael that he was a thoughtful and caring friend.

What would have been the right way to handle this situation? Richard should have known that Michael would appreciate his phone call, regardless of how many other calls he received. During times of tragedy, people become more sensitive to and aware of the generosity and compassion others show them. If you have ever suffered through an illness or the death of someone close to you, I'm sure you remember how much you appreciated and valued the support of your friends and family at that time. Making a phone call to a person in a difficult time is of utmost importance.

Richard could have called Michael to offer his condolences with a few brief yet meaningful comments—"I'm sorry to hear about your mother. This must be a very difficult time for you"—and then shifted the focus of the conversation to what he could do to help—"Is there anything I can do to help?" Combining his condolences with an offer of help is a communication wonder because it would have given Michael the chance to talk about the loss of his mother and then move on to the less emotional topic of whether there was anything his friend could do to help. Whenever someone you care about is suffering from an illness or mourning the loss of someone close, there is one thing you must be sure to do. Make that difficult phone call. Express your sympathy and then offer your help.

•   •   •   •   •

COMMUNICATION WONDER

Create Comfort in a Difficult Time

When someone you care about is ill or mourning the loss of someone, always call that person. Say, "This must be a difficult time for you. Is there anything I can do to help?"

Rule 25

· · · · ·

Ask
and You'll
Receive

A MAJOR OBSTACLE TO getting what we want is often nothing more than a roadblock we create ourselves. Yes, that's right. We get in our own way and hamper our success. We tell ourselves things like, "If my boss wanted to give me a raise, he would, so I guess I shouldn't ask him for it." "If it were possible, it would would have already been done." "If my colleague wanted to give me her old couch, she would have offered it to me." You may decide not to ask for any of these things in spite of the fact that you want it because you convince yourself that you won't get it anyway and you don't want to place yourself in an awkward or uncomfortable position by asking for it. So what do you do? You play it safe. You walk away from the situation believing that if the person wanted you to have it, he would have offered it to you.

Yet there is a fundamental flaw in this thinking because you can never be sure why someone doesn't offer you something. It is certainly possible that he doesn't want to give it to you, but it is also quite possible that he hasn't given a moment's thought to you and what you want, or he may simply be waiting for you to ask him for it. Your boss doesn't wake up in the morning thinking about your raise, but you do. And maybe your colleague thinks she would insult you if she offered to give you her used furniture. For all the times in the past that you didn't ask for something, you probably missed many opportunities to get exactly what you wanted.

Today I challenge you to think differently. Begin by thinking about these questions: Do you make the effort to ask for what you want even when you think the answer will be no? Are you afraid of getting a no answer? Do you avoid taking a long shot by asking for something you want because you think it will be a waste of time and energy? In the following stories you will see that when you don't make the effort to ask for something, you miss the chance to get people to cooperate with you and give you exactly what you want.

One Thursday evening Herb went to the movies with two friends, Ken and Douglass. This was the first time they had been out together without their wives. They bought their tickets at the theater and went across the street to a pizza shop to eat something before the movie. As they ate they joked about how none of their wives had any interest in seeing the type of movie they were about to see. "Well," Ken said, "I have to say, I think I'm a pretty lucky man. Even though my wife doesn't like science fiction movies, she does like basketball. This year

I bought season tickets to the Knicks and she actually enjoys going to the games with me." "You have season tickets?" Herb asked. "Wow, that's great. I'm a Knicks fan, too." "Well, to be honest," Ken responded, "I decided to purchase the season tickets for two reasons: business and pleasure. My customers are so grateful when I offer them the tickets. I usually give them away when my wife and I can't make it to a game." "I'll bet that's good for business," Herb commented. He continued, "I heard the playoff game on Wednesday is going to be really hot. It sold out in a couple hours." "You're right. It's going to be a great game," Ken agreed, "but the worst thing is I won't be able to go because my son's school play is next Wednesday night, so that's where we'll be."

"Oh, that's awful," Herb said, envisioning the two empty seats at the game. Herb honestly felt bad for Ken for missing such an important game, but at the same time he hoped Ken would say something like, "Well, Herb, since I can't go to the game, do you want the tickets?" But Ken said nothing like that and the conversation shifted to another topic. "Oh well," Herb thought to himself, "I really want those tickets and I would gladly pay for them, but I feel uncomfortable asking for them. Ken already said that he gives them away to his customers. I suspect that if he wanted me to have the tickets, he would have offered them to me." By the time Herb finished this negative self-talk, he had concluded that Ken had other plans for the tickets so it would be wise for him to remain silent and forget about going to the game.

Ken, Herb and Douglass left the restaurant and crossed the street to the movie theater. Just when they were about to walk inside, Douglass casually said, "Hey, Ken, I was thinking, since you're not going to the Knicks game on Wednesday, can

I buy the tickets from you?" Herb was surprised that Douglass asked for the tickets. He expected Ken to say no to Douglass for the same reasons he was sure Ken would have said no to him. So when Ken smiled and said, "Doug, the tickets are all yours," Herb was stunned. He said nothing as he walked into the movie theater angry with himself for not asking Ken for what he wanted and disappointed that he wasn't going to this incredible Knicks game.

Herb made a communication blunder when he let his personal concerns stop him from taking a shot at asking for what he wanted. He wrongly assumed that Ken would offer him the tickets if he wanted him to have them. However, Herb didn't realize that Ken wasn't thinking about what to do with the unused tickets or whether or not Herb would want them. He was thinking about himself and how he had to miss the game to go to a school play. As it turned out, Ken was happy to sell the tickets to one of his friends. All he needed was for someone to ask him for them.

> **COMMUNICATION BLUNDER**
>
> It's a blunder to expect someone to offer you something that you want.

In the next story you will see how I got exactly what I wanted by taking a long shot. When I was at Harvard Law School I worked as a mediator, helping people resolve their legal disputes. I found mediation personally rewarding and very helpful to the clients with whom I worked. So when I graduated and moved to New York City, my plan was to continue acting as a volunteer mediator in the New York City court system while I focused on my legal career at a corporate law firm. Within weeks of starting my legal practice, I reviewed the literature on the firm's pro bono program, in which the lawyers are encouraged to work with nonprofit organizations to provide free legal services to people who are unable to pay for their own legal representation. After reading the paperwork thoroughly, I was disappointed to discover that the pro bono program didn't seem broad enough to include mediation work. I spoke about this to another associate who had worked at the firm for a few years. He said, "Our firm has a well-established pro bono program, but you're right, mediation hasn't been a part of it. I suspect that if they wanted to include mediation in the pro bono work you would have found it in the program description." I was discouraged. I thought, "He's probably right, there has to be a good reason why the firm isn't offering mediation services in their pro bono program." I sat in my office staring at the papers that described the pro bono program, unhappy that I wouldn't be able to continue working in the field of mediation.

Suddenly, I had a light bulb moment! "Aha," I thought. "Why am I giving up on this idea? Is it because I expect the firm to offer me exactly what I want?" I was accepting the idea that I wouldn't be able to practice mediation even though I didn't know of any valid reason why it wasn't being offered. I thought, "If it's not offered now, then it probably won't be offered in the future, unless someone like me requests it. Asking to mediate might be a long shot, but what's the worst thing that could happen? I could be told no and I'd be in the same position I'm in now, unable to mediate." I had nothing to lose and everything to gain. Convinced and reinvigorated, I decided to move forward in pursuit of my goal.

The next morning I went to see the partner in charge of the pro bono program. She was an approachable woman and I thought I might have a chance of getting her approval for me to mediate. I asked her, "Is this a good time for you to talk to me about the pro bono program?" "Sure," she said, "have a seat." I sat down and calmly asked, "Is mediation presently offered as an option in the firm's pro bono program?" I hoped she would say yes so that our conversation would be over and I would have what I wanted, but she said no. Gathering up my courage, I continued, "Can I ask you why not?" "To tell you the truth, up until now no one's ever asked to be a mediator," she replied matter-of-factly. "It's not the kind of pro bono work that our lawyers usually do." "Oh," I said, "then I suppose I may be the first one who wants to do it. I know that mediation would provide an important legal service to the community. I checked and there is an existing mediation program being offered at a nearby courthouse and I'd like to volunteer there. So what do you think about including mediation in the pro bono program?" I paused, waiting for her response. "I don't see why not," she said. "It sounds like a good idea. Mediation is a valuable process for resolving conflicts. It's even possible that some other lawyers here would want to do it, too. Why don't you draft a letter of engagement and have the director of the mediation program at the court sign it and return it to me so we can get it going." "Okay, I'll get right on it," I said. "Thank you for your help." I got up and joyfully walked out of her office.

At that moment I realized that I had almost missed the chance to get what I wanted. I had almost convinced myself that because pro bono mediation was not offered at the firm at that time, I wouldn't be able to do it. How foolish of me! By asking for mediation to be included in the program, I got what I wanted and I gave other lawyers in the firm an opportunity to become involved in mediation as well. With the courage to ask a question that seemed like a long shot, I turned the whole situation around. This experience motivated me to create a simple yet profound communication wonder that continues to make a positive difference in my life every day. Use this wonder, based on a simple concept—if you don't ask, you won't receive, but if you do ask, you might receive—to make a positive difference in your life.

COMMUNICATION WONDER

Ask and You'll Receive

When you want something, ask for it. People don't know what you want, only you do.

Rule 26

· · · · ·

Earn
Your
Favors

WE ALL NEED HELP sometimes. Chances are you've asked someone for a favor in the past and you'll ask a favor of someone in the future. But when you ask for a favor at the wrong time under the wrong circumstances, you risk being perceived as a "user" and creating resentment and antagonism in a relationship. In fact, by unwittingly asking for a favor under the wrong circumstances you can virtually be assured that the person you're asking will be uncooperative. So is there a way to ensure that the circumstances are right to ask for a favor? The answer is a simple yes.

The best way to get what you want is to persuade someone to cooperate with you by making him a friend, not a resource.

Over time, when you treat someone like a friend by letting him know that you have a sincere interest in his well-being, you put yourself in line to earn a favor. Similarly, when someone treats you well, you are willing to go out of your way to lend him a helping hand. In the stories below you will see how asking for a favor under the wrong circumstances is a communication blunder because it makes a person feel used. Then you will learn the communication wonder that enhances a relationship so that the person you are asking for a favor wants to give you what you want.

Imagine that you like your job as a computer technician, but you want to earn more money and have greater managerial control. You decide to look around for a position in your specialty, but at a company where you might be able to take a step up in pay and title. You look through the help wanted ads and find a bunch of jobs that interest you. One is at a company where your friend Evan is employed in the human resources department. You haven't thought about Evan for quite some time because you've been busy, but now that you need something from him you figure it's a good time to give him a call. You remember that he put in a good word for another friend who applied for a job there almost two years ago. You hope that he will be willing to do the same for you.

You call Evan and can tell that he's happy to hear from you. You chat briefly about what's going on in your lives and then you tell him why you suddenly thought of him. "I saw an advertisement for a position at your company and I'm interested in applying for it. It says to apply through the human resources department so I thought you could personally hand in my résumé and recommend me to the person in charge of filling that position." To Evan, this request is quite revealing. He now fully understands that the only reason you called him was to use him for a favor, not to rekindle the friendship. Since he knows you have no interest in him, he has no interest in putting himself out to make it easier for you to get a job. So he says, "I'm sorry, I won't be able to help you out. I'm not in a position to make any employment recommendations." You are surprised by this response. "But haven't you done that before? Can't you just hand in my résumé so I know it gets into the right hands?" "No, I'm sorry. I can't," he quickly responds. "Just send it in like everyone else." "Okay," you say, believing that he could help you out if he wanted to. As you hang up the phone you're thinking that Evan used to be a nice guy but he isn't anymore, while Evan is thinking that you have some nerve calling him out of the blue just to ask him for a favor.

Although it may seem like the conversation went sour because Evan was being selfish and unhelpful, the truth is that it was you who made the communication blunder that turned the conversation sour when you treated Evan like a resource instead of a friend. While Evan could have helped you out if he wanted to, he didn't want to because people choose to do favors for people who earn them. With Evan, you hadn't earned any favors.

COMMUNICATION BLUNDER

It is a blunder to expect someone to do a favor for you when you haven't maintained a consistent relationship with that person.

The next story illustrates in more detail how asking someone for a favor when you haven't maintained a relationship
with that person prevents you from getting what you want.
Then you will see how a communication wonder easily works
to persuade people to cooperate with you.

One evening during dinner Melissa's husband says he thinks
it's time to buy a new Italian leather couch for their living
room. Melissa agrees with him because the fabric on their old
couch is so worn out she's sure it's going to rip soon. Melissa's
husband suggests that she call Jaime, a friend and former
neighbor who works for a leather furniture company. He
thinks Jaime might be able to get them a discount on a quality couch. Melissa agrees and thinks that this might also be
a good opportunity to reconnect with Jaime because they
haven't been in touch since Jaime moved a year before.

When the dinner table is cleared, Melissa calls Jaime, hoping that she's home, but more important, hoping that she still
works for the furniture company. Jaime answers. "Hi, Melissa.
It's nice to hear from you after such a long time. To what do I
owe this phone call?" Jaime asks. "Well, I just called to say hello.
So tell me, how are you?" "Well, I can't complain. Things are
going well," Jaime says. "The kids are great and I was recently
promoted to vice president at the furniture company. And how
is everything with you and your family?" Melissa says, "Everything is fine, but I was actually wondering if I could buy a
leather couch through you at a discount." Jaime is silent for a
moment. She sees the situation for what it is. She recognizes
that Melissa didn't call her to keep in touch; she was only calling for a couch. Jaime thinks, "It would have been nice to see
Melissa again. I probably should have called her myself. But
for Melissa to call me now, after all this time, just to get a dis-

count on a couch is disappointing and offensive. What nerve! I don't like that she's trying to take advantage of me. It makes me feel used."

Although Jaime knows that she could easily do this favor for Melissa, she won't because she's angry and Melissa hasn't earned the favor. Jaime doesn't want to be rude and say "absolutely not" so she decides to give her a more ambiguous answer. "Well, I wish I could help you out, but my company's policy is very strict about this. I won't be able to get you a discount." "Oh," Melissa says. "If I remember correctly, you used to be able to get discounts." "Well, that was a long time ago. The company policy has changed since we last spoke. I can't get discounts for anyone except immediate family. Sorry, but it's getting late and I have to get my kids ready for bed. We'll talk again sometime." They hang up and Melissa is disappointed by Jaime's unfriendly, uncooperative attitude. Melissa thinks to herself, "It only goes to show how selfish some people can be. It wouldn't have cost her anything to be nice to me."

What happened here? Melissa misread the situation. It's not that Jaime is selfish and won't go out of her way for others. It's that Jaime won't go out of her way for Melissa. Melissa made a communication blunder when she asked Jaime for a favor even though she hadn't seen or spoken to her for a long time. Melissa didn't realize that friendship is a two-way street.

What should Melissa have done? In this case, Melissa should not have asked Jaime for a favor because Melissa hadn't kept up their friendship. Many of us lose touch with friends, family members and colleagues until we need something from them, which prompts us to call them. But reconnecting only because we need a favor makes other people feel like they are being used. Not surprisingly, this is the surest way to persuade others *not* to give us what we want.

Making a point of keeping in touch with certain people when we don't need anything is the surest way to show them that we genuinely care about them, and in turn they will genuinely care about us. This type of genuine relationship encourages people to want to help each other out at all times, especially when they need a favor. If Melissa had made a point of connecting with Jaime after her move, at a time when she didn't need anything from her, then Jaime would have been happy to help Melissa get a discount later on.

One simple thing that I do to make sure that I don't "forget to connect" is to write down in my datebook the names of my friends, family members and colleagues with whom I don't want to lose contact simply because of distance and my active schedule. Sporadically I look at this list and make phone calls just to keep in touch. Once you make sure that you don't forget to connect, you will enjoy more rewarding relationships with others and you will put yourself in line to earn many more favors.

COMMUNICATION WONDER

Earn Your Favors

Don't forget to connect. Show an interest in people when you don't need anything from them.

Rule 27

· · · · ·

Disagree Without Being Disagreeable

DO YOU EXPRESS AN opposing view in a way that persuades someone to listen to you or ignore you? If someone tells you his opinion and you disagree, how do you respond? Do you say, without a moment's hesitation, "I disagree with you"? Do you then immediately begin to explain your opinion? Do you give the other person a chance to explain himself? It may surprise you, but there are different ways to respond to someone with whom you disagree. The way you choose to respond affects what you get out of the situation. If you view a difference of opinion as a competition that you want to win by having the last word, then you can respond any way you want. However, if you want to build a relationship based on mutual respect and cooperation, then there is an effective communication wonder that you should employ to disagree. The communication wonder in this chapter shows you how to disagree without being disagreeable, to enable you to avoid unnecessary conflict and persuade people to listen to and respect you. It is all too easy for two people with differing opinions to turn a calm situation into one of conflict. Let's see how this happens.

For the past four years, ever since their youngest son went away to college, Sharon and Bruce have set aside time in September to take a two-week vacation somewhere outside the United States. One day in March, Sharon sees her friend Connie at the gym. Knowing that Connie and her husband are frequent travelers, Sharon asks her for a travel suggestion. Connie immediately recommends Australia, where she and her husband went last year and had a fantastic time. Since Sharon and Bruce have never been to Australia, Sharon returns home from the gym and goes to her computer to do some Internet research on the country. By the time she finishes printing out descriptions of cities and pictures of the national parks, beaches and cultural attractions, Sharon has made her decision. Connie was right, Australia seems like the perfect place to vacation.

That evening as Sharon and Bruce are having dinner Sharon says, "Bruce, I think it's time we talk about where we want to go on vacation this September. I want to start looking into the hotel and airfare prices early so I have enough time to get us a good deal." "Funny you should bring that up tonight," says Bruce. "I was just thinking about the same thing. Do you have any ideas?" "Actually, I do," Sharon answers happily. "I talked to a friend at the gym today and after doing some research on the Internet, I think we should go to Australia." Bruce doesn't want to go to Australia. "No, no way," he automatically responds. "I have no intention of sitting on a plane for twenty hours, going all the way from New York to Australia, just to see a kangaroo. There's nothing great about that place anyway. I want to go to Scotland." Sharon is instantly irritated with Bruce for dismissing her opinion without asking her why she wants to go to Australia. So when Bruce starts to explain why he wants to go to Scotland, Sharon pays no attention because she is too busy planning her counterattack.

Seconds later, she interrupts him. "You don't know anything about Australia. You've never been there. So how can you possibly say there is nothing to do there?" Now Bruce, agitated by Sharon's interruption, repeats what he said about Scotland in a louder, more forceful voice. "There is a lot more to do in Scotland. Like I said before, it would be much more exciting to go there because in addition to the sightseeing we could play some of Scotland's world-famous golf courses. Not to mention that Scotland is a lot closer so we won't have to waste so much time traveling." Fuming at Bruce's close-mindedness, Sharon responds by attacking his opinion. "Well, I don't want to go to Scotland. I'm not that interested in golf. You play enough golf right here so why should I travel all the way to Scotland just so you can play more golf? Let's just scrap our vacation plans and you can play golf here all you want!"

Bruce knows that Sharon is being disagreeable out of spite and that bothers him. "You're only saying that because I won't go to Australia and you're not getting your way. I don't know why you get so upset with me every time I disagree with you," Bruce exclaims. "What do you expect me to do?" asks Sharon, "agree with everything you say and keep my mouth shut?" "No," replies Bruce. "You're entitled to your opinion, but so am I." "Well, maybe if you practiced what you preached and gave me a chance to explain my opinion, I would listen to what you have to say," announces Sharon.

It was certainly acceptable for Bruce to have an opinion, but what was not acceptable was the way he chose to express it. Bruce made a communication blunder when he automatically said no to Sharon's suggestion. His quick and thoughtless dismissal of her opinion sent Sharon the message that both she and her idea were worthless. Feeling disrespected by Bruce, Sharon became resentful and refused to listen to anything he had to say. In the end, they didn't come to an agreement.

COMMUNICATION BLUNDER

When someone has an opinion, it is a blunder to automatically disagree with that opinion before you take the time to consider it.

See what happened when Diane, head of the science department at a public high school in Philadelphia, automatically dismissed an idea that Martha, a teacher, offered. Both Diane and Martha were science teachers at the school until the previous year, when Diane became Martha's boss after being promoted to head of the department. Since Diane's promotion, the enthusiasm of the science teachers has steadily waned. Martha and some of the other science teachers often talked about Diane over lunch. They all agreed that she was not as effective as the previous department head because she seldom paid attention to the teachers' ideas and opinions. Diane's non-inclusive leadership style frustrated and alienated the teachers in the department. Many of them no longer bothered to offer Diane suggestions for ways to strengthen the science curriculum and increase efficiency in the department. Martha, who was a dedicated teacher, was one of the few teachers who still kept trying to work with Diane, despite Diane's authoritative style.

One afternoon after the school day ended, Martha sat at her desk preparing her lesson plans for the following week. She was waiting for Diane to return from a district department head meeting so she could talk to her about an idea for a new science program. A few days earlier Martha had discovered an interesting article in the newspaper about a science program that had been implemented in a nearby high school. It mentioned the name of a student in the program who was chosen as a finalist in the Intel Science Talent Search science fair competition. Martha thought that offering the students at her school the same program with the opportunity to design projects and enter them in such a prestigious competition would be a wonderful educational experience for them. She knew that if a student participated in this type of science program it would be a real plus on his or her college application. Martha also expected that if one of the students actually won the science fair competition, it not only would benefit the student, but also would give the science department special recognition, which could result in a larger annual budget for the department. For all these reasons, Martha was excited about the program and decided she would volunteer her time to develop it and work with students who showed interest in entering it.

When Martha heard Diane's voice in the hall, she eagerly got up from her desk and walked across the hall to Diane's office. "Do you have a few minutes?" Martha asked. "Yes, come in," Diane replied. Martha took the newspaper article out of her pocket and began to present her idea. Holding the article, she said, "I read this article and I think it would be a great idea for our school to offer a similar science program to our students." Martha had barely finished her sentence when Diane automatically responded. "No. We can't do it. We don't have the money to try anything new. I believe we should allocate our funds to things that benefit all of the students, not just those special few who excel." Martha instantly felt annoyed and frustrated because Diane had rudely dismissed her idea without listening to any of her reasons for supporting Martha's idea. Diane recognized the frustration on Martha's face, so she went on to elaborate on her reasons for rejecting Martha's idea, hoping to convince Martha that she was right. "Martha, putting aside the cost, there is no interest in this kind of program at this school. Not one student, teacher or parent has brought the Intel competition to my attention before today. We already offer our students many excellent programs. I don't see any reason for the science department to add anything at this time. Is there something else you want to discuss?" "No, you've said it all," replied Martha. Diane's display of disrespect and indifference toward her idea was the final straw for Martha. That day she decided not to waste any more of her valuable time suggesting new ideas.

Diane made a communication blunder that instantly persuaded Martha to resent her. What was Diane's mistake? Diane disagreed with Martha and didn't even give her a chance to explain her idea before rejecting it. Diane wasn't interested in looking at the newspaper article and she did not ask Martha to explain her reasons for advocating a new science program. By rejecting Martha's opinion without giving it any consideration, Diane sent Martha the message that she didn't respect her or value her ideas. Diane's instant negativity discouraged Martha from sharing ideas in the future that could benefit the students, the science department and the school. Diane's habit of quickly dismissing opposing views weakened her authority and limited progress in the science department.

In contrast, if Diane had a habit of listening to other people's ideas, she would have made the teachers in her department feel important and valued. In this situation, Diane should have used a communication wonder and waited to express her opinion until she had specifically asked Martha, "What are your reasons for saying that?" and listened to her answer. If Diane had done that, Martha would have felt as though she was part of the decision-making process and Diane would have received information that would have allowed her to weigh the pros and cons of Martha's idea. For one thing, Diane would have learned that Martha was willing to volunteer her time to supervise the program. Even if Diane still disagreed with Martha's opinion after listening to her points, she would have at least given Martha the respect she deserved by allowing her to be heard. In turn, Martha would have respected Diane and her final decision even though she disagreed with it.

Automatically dismissing a person's opinion without giving him the opportunity to be heard is a sure way to turn people off and get yourself disliked and disrespected. It's okay to disagree with someone, but the way you choose to disagree matters. Use this wonder to achieve communication breakthroughs instead of communication breakdowns so that you arrive at mutually agreeable conclusions with others.

COMMUNICATION WONDER

Disagree Without Being Disagreeable

Before you disagree with someone's opinion, ask, "What are your reasons for saying that?" Listen to his answer *before* you respond.

Rule 28

· · · · ·

Be a Party-Wise Host

WHAT CAN YOU DO to make sure that every party you throw is extraordinary, not ordinary? Well, to start, you can obviously provide good food and drinks. But there is something else, something less obvious, that you should offer your guests to make your party extraordinary. It is free yet priceless. It is taking the time to talk to your guests to make them feel important and connected to the other guests.

Any party-wise host realizes that invitations are not requests for presents or personal attention. They are requests for guests to come together to socialize and create and recharge relationships. When a person is deciding whether or not to accept your party invitation, he or she will probably think about who else will be there. The most memorable and enjoyable parties are those at which guests feel important and meet new, friendly and interesting people. As a party-wise host you should be aware of this so that the next time you host a party you view your role as that of a "people connector," to set the stage for an extraordinary party at which guests like you and one another.

In the stories below you will see what happens at a party when a host narrowly centers the party around herself. Then you will discover what happens at another party when a host broadens her attention to include her guests by acting as a people connector.

Rebecca, a high-powered attorney, recently moved into a new apartment in a modern building in the center of Boston. The apartment has a living room, den, bedroom and a private outdoor patio with a garden. Rebecca decides that summer is an opportune time to host a housewarming party to show off her new place and reconnect with some of her friends. She invites thirty people, including her college and law school friends who live in the area, some neighbors in her building and various colleagues from her law firm. Over the next month, Rebecca spends a lot of time preparing for the party. She mails out invitations and hires someone to help her on the night of the party. She orders platters of food and stocks the bar. Rebecca plants flowers in her garden and buys special lanterns to create a unique patio atmosphere. She even buys some interesting artwork for her walls so that her apartment will look impressive when everyone sees it for the first time. She is confident that all of these extras will make her party a success.

When the night of the big event arrives, with all the preparations done, Rebecca is ready to enjoy herself and be a

guest at her own party. She greets the first guest, her neighbor
Jack. Rebecca hopes that inviting Jack will be the beginning
of a friendly relationship between them. She takes his housewarming gift, thanks him and shows him to the food, where
she talks to him for a minute. "Aren't the apartments in this
building great?" Rebecca asks. "Yes," Jack says, looking
around. "You know, my apartment has the same layout as
yours but without the patio. I went for a minimalist look, but
I like your contemporary style." "Thanks," says Rebecca, who
hears a knock at the door and announces, "I'll be right back."
Jack nibbles on shrimp cocktail and waits for Rebecca to return with the guests who just arrived. A couple minutes pass
and Jack notices that Rebecca is engrossed in a conversation
with a group of friends. It seems like she isn't going to introduce him to anyone and he is on his own. He feels uncomfortable walking over to Rebecca and inviting himself into her
conversation, so he gets a drink and walks outside to take a
closer look at the patio.

After ten minutes, he wanders back inside and spots Rebecca still talking to the same group of people near the front
door. This time he walks up to the group and listens to them
talking about a recent legal decision. Rebecca sees Jack but
doesn't acknowledge his presence or introduce him to the
group. After a while Jack, uninvolved, bored and tired, slips
out of the party to return to his apartment. Not surprisingly,
Rebecca doesn't notice Jack's departure because she is too
busy entertaining herself with her friends. In fact, Rebecca
has even stopped noticing who arrives because she left her
front door open so she wouldn't have to interrupt her conversations to greet her guests at the door.

Time passes and Rebecca is very happy. She looks around

and is pleased that so many people think enough of her to come to her party. She confidently walks over to her college friends who are busy talking about her apartment and her excellent decorating taste. "Your apartment is beautiful," her friend Susan says to her. "I didn't know you had such decorating talent." "Thanks," Rebecca replies, and then eagerly goes on to talk about the decorating magazines she's been reading. Rebecca talks with her college friends about the good old days until it's time to refresh her drink. She leaves to get a drink and joins in on the conversation with her law school friends near the bar. As she pours herself some wine one of her law school friends asks, "Who were you just talking to?" "Oh, those are my friends from college," she says. Rebecca stays by the bar talking to her law school friends until one of them suggests that they all head outside to sit on the patio. There, she sees some of her colleagues, but doesn't think to introduce them to the group of law school friends.

Rebecca thinks she is being a good host and that her party is a success. But her party is not as good as it could be because her guests are not connecting to one another. Rebecca has been busy taking care of herself instead of her guests. As a result her party has turned into many separate little parties instead of what she wanted—one big friendly housewarming party. In the end, many of her guests will go home thinking that they had a nice time, but might have had an equally nice time sitting at a bar talking to the friends they came with.

Rebecca made a communication blunder every time she failed to make a guest feel important by introducing him to other guests and helping him get involved in conversations. Rebecca made the mistake of acting like a guest at her own party, instead of the host. She assumed everyone would take care of themselves and mix and mingle on their own. Unfortunately, what Rebecca didn't realize was that it can be awkward to leave a conversation with people you know to move on and possibly intrude on a conversation with people you don't know. This is why people appreciate a host who helps them break the ice. Rebecca didn't foster a warm, friendly atmosphere at her party because she spent too much time connecting herself to others instead of connecting her guests to one another.

COMMUNICATION BLUNDER

It is a blunder to think that the job of a party host ends when the guests arrive.

I recently attended an extraordinary holiday party hosted by my friend Liz. Liz clearly understood her role as a people connector. From the moment I arrived, Liz made me feel important and welcome. Here is what she did to make her party extraordinary:

I arrived at the party with a bottle of wine in hand. Liz opened the door and smiled. "Hi, Laurie, I'm so happy you could make it." I instantly felt that she cared about my presence at her party. "I'm glad you invited me," I responded. "Here's something for you." I handed her the wine. "Thanks so much," Liz said. "Let me take your coat." Liz put the wine on the table, took my coat and hung it in the closet. As she did, I quickly glanced around the apartment looking for people I knew. I noticed a few of my friends standing near the kitchen, so I planned to walk over to them as soon as Liz finished welcoming me. Yet, surprisingly, even though Liz knew that I had some friends at the party, she asked, "Laurie, do you know everyone here?" I looked around and said, "No, I don't know the group of people by the drinks." "Oh, those are my friends from work. Let me introduce you to them." Liz walked me over to them and said, "Hi, I want you to meet my friend Laurie. This is Susanna, Marisa and John, some of my friends from work. Laurie is writing a self-help book about persuasion. Isn't that amazing?" I turned and smiled at Liz. Hosts rarely take the time to introduce people in such a meaningful way, and at that moment Liz made me feel important and comfortable at her party. Conversation with my new acquaintances quickly took off. They asked me about my book and I asked them about their interests. Liz was an active participant in the conversation until the doorbell rang. Seeing that everyone was involved in the conversation, she walked away to welcome the next guest.

As the evening went on, Liz made a point of welcoming her guests as they arrived. She made sure that circles of friends intermingled and encouraged people to connect and get to know one another by introducing individuals and groups to one another. She created crossover conversations to build bridges among her friends. When Liz looked around and noticed someone standing alone, she took the time to talk to that person and bring him or her into a conversation with other people. Within a short period of time everyone at Liz's party was smiling, friendly and felt connected to others. It was obvious that Liz's party was a huge success because of the warm, friendly atmosphere she had created. As people left the party that night I overheard them thanking Liz for a fantastic party. They didn't comment on the food, the drinks or the decorations; they commented on what a wonderful host Liz was and how much they had enjoyed meeting her friends.

Liz knew how to make her guests feel important and comfortable. She understood that people come to a party to meet new people and enjoy themselves, not to spend the evening talking only to the host or to people they already know. Liz used a communication wonder to make her party memorable and extraordinary. She gave her guests what they wanted—her attention, involvement and thoughtful introductions—to enable them to easily and comfortably meet new people. Liz instantly persuaded her guests to appreciate and like her for bringing them together. Her warmth and social grace were reflected in the success of the party.

The next time you host a party, remember that the key to having a lively, friendly and successful party is to say the right words at the right time to make your guests feel welcome, important and connected to you and one another.

COMMUNICATION WONDER

Be a Party-Wise Host

When hosting a party, be a people connector. Make your guests feel important by taking the time to introduce them and initiate conversations.

Rule 29

· · · · ·

Don't Cave Under Pressure

WHAT DO YOU SAY when a friend, family member or colleague is pressuring you for an immediate answer or decision and you don't know what to say? Do you give him a quick yes or no answer only to regret it afterward? Giving someone a final answer under pressure when you haven't had time to think it over is a communication blunder. You are likely to say something that causes you and others unnecessary stress and conflict. The following stories illustrate how caving under pressure is a communication blunder. Then you will learn how to successfully handle tough situations like this in the future.

It's the end of November and Amanda is in her cozy studio apartment in Manhattan. She is relaxing and polishing her nails one Sunday afternoon when her mother calls. "Hi, sweetie. How are you?" "I'm fine, Mom. What's up?" Amanda's parents live in Philadelphia, a two-hour drive from Amanda's apartment. She sees them once in a while and talks to her mother on the phone a few times a week. "Well," her mother says, "I'm calling because I just got off the phone with my brother Joe. His family isn't going to his in-laws' for Christmas this year. Instead he's considering taking his family to Aruba for vacation. I told him that since he isn't going to his in-laws', maybe I would make Christmas dinner for the whole family. He said he would rather spend Christmas with us than go away. So I told him I wanted to talk to you first to find out if you would come home and help me with the dinner and then I would get back to him. You know, you haven't been home for Christmas in a long time. The years are flying by and we're all getting older, especially your grandmother. It would be nice if you spent more time with her. Joe is waiting for me to call him back with my answer so he can make plans. So will you come home for Christmas?"

Amanda feels pressured to say yes because she wants to make her mother happy. But she wants to say no because she has tentative plans to go skiing in Vermont with three of her friends over the Christmas holiday. Amanda hasn't been skiing in years and she really enjoys it. She told her friends to count her in for the ski trip, but Brooke, who was supposed to plan it, hasn't called her to confirm anything since the four of them talked about the trip a few weeks ago. Amanda knows there is a good chance that the ski trip won't materialize.

Under pressure from her mother for an answer, Amanda caves in and says, "Okay, I'll come." Amanda's mother is thrilled. "Great. I'll call Joe back right now to tell him we're on. I'll call you tomorrow." Later that day Amanda calls Brooke to let her know that her Christmas plans have changed and she can't go skiing, but Brooke isn't home so she leaves a message asking Brooke to call her back.

To Amanda's surprise, the next day Brooke returns her call and is all excited because she was able to get a reservation for a suite for all four of them in one of the inns in Stratton, Vermont. Amanda is not happy because now she's going to have to disappoint her friends. If she were given the choice all over again, Amanda would have chosen to go on the ski trip rather than see her family, whom she can see at another time. Regretfully, Amanda tells Brooke, "I know I told you I wanted to go to Vermont, but I can't go anymore. I agreed to go to my parents' house for Christmas because I assumed the ski trip was off since I hadn't heard from you." "What? I spent hours calling places to arrange for us to go skiing. I finally found a suite and gave a deposit over the phone, expecting that the four of us would share the cost. You can't imagine how many phone calls I had to make before I found this place. Why would you assume that we weren't going without talking to me first? It's not like Christmas is next week. It's only the end of November." "I know, you're right. I shouldn't have agreed to go to my parents' house so quickly, but my mom needed an answer right away, so I had to make a quick decision." "Why don't you call your mother and tell her that you changed your mind?" "I wish I could," Amanda answers, "but I promised to help her prepare dinner. And she's already invited my grandmother and my uncle's family, so I can't back out now." Brooke is offended. "Well, it sure was easy for you to back out of the plans with me. I don't know what the three of us are going to do now with a suite for four." Distressed, Amanda says, "I'm really sorry. Maybe you can switch to a different room." Their conversation ends on a bad note.

Amanda made a communication blunder when she caved under pressure from her mother and gave a final answer despite her misgivings. Amanda responded as if there was a deadline in place when there wasn't. Her mother and Uncle Joe could have waited a few days to finalize their Christmas plans. Unfortunately, Amanda didn't know how to give a polite answer that wasn't yes or no.

COMMUNICATION BLUNDER

It is a blunder to cave under pressure and give someone a final answer before you are prepared to do so.

There is a simple way to avoid this communication blunder. In the next story you see how Marilyn could have avoided a communication blunder by using a communication wonder.

Marilyn is an active member of the Sisterhood at a temple in Long Island, New York. The Sisterhood organizes educational and social events at the temple for members. When Marilyn moved to the community last year, she joined the group and made many new friends, including Joan, the president.

Tonight, Marilyn is attending a Sisterhood meeting. On the agenda is an idea for a monthly speaker series. Joan introduces the idea and asks everyone for their opinion. There are a dozen women at the meeting and every one of them, including Marilyn, agrees that it is a good idea because it would significantly add to the educational programming already in place. After they agree to start a monthly speaker series, Marilyn makes a suggestion. "I think we should pick a regular day and time for the program, like the first Tuesday of every month at eight P.M., so people can plan to attend well in advance." "That's a good idea," Joan responds. "You know, we need someone to be the chairperson of the speaker series. Marilyn, I think you would be perfect since you always have so many great ideas. Will you chair the committee?"

Marilyn doesn't know what to say. Everyone is staring at her, waiting for her response. Marilyn feels flattered by Joan's compliment, but unsure about accepting this time-consuming position. With all eyes on her, Marilyn feels enormous pressure to make a decision. Uncomfortable and stressed, she says, "Okay." Joan smiles and says, "Great. Anyone who wants to work with Marilyn on the speaker series should talk to her after the meeting. Let's move on to the next item on the agenda."

By the end of the meeting, Marilyn regrets her decision. She caved under the pressure of the moment when she gave Joan a final answer. Marilyn thinks to herself, "I love being part of the Sisterhood, but with two young kids at home, I'm incredibly busy. It's going to be difficult for me to organize, advertise and attend every event. I don't know how I got myself into this, but I did. Now I can't go back on my word. If I do, I'll look irresponsible and unreliable."

Marilyn made a communication blunder when she caved under Joan's pressure and gave her a final answer when she wasn't prepared to. Marilyn incorrectly assumed that she had to give her answer then and there, even though there was no urgency or deadline. Unfortunately, Marilyn saw only two ways to respond to Joan's request: to say yes or no. But Marilyn had a third choice and a better way to respond.

Instead of saying yes or no to Joan, Marilyn's response should have consisted of two parts: (1) "Let me think about it," and (2) "I'll get back to you with my decision tomorrow." The second comment, which sets a self-imposed deadline, would have shown Joan that Marilyn respects her request, her time and her need for an answer, even though she can't provide it at that moment.

It's okay to delay a decision as long as you set a reasonable deadline for yourself, depending on the situation you find yourself in. It is essential that you meet your self-imposed deadline to be reliable and responsible. Take the time you need to make a well-thought-out decision so you can stand by your word and persuade others to trust and respect what you say.

COMMUNICATION WONDER

Don't Cave Under Pressure

When you are not sure of your answer to a question, the appropriate and decisive response is: "Let me think about it. I'll get back to you by _____ [fill in with a specific day and/or time]."

Rule 30

· · · · ·

Keep It Private

NAOMI DIDN'T KNOW SHE wasn't supposed to tell anyone about it. How could she? Her friend Michelle didn't tell her to keep her lips sealed when she said, "I made an appointment to see a psychologist next week. I plan to see her for just a few months. I have a couple of things to work out, nothing major, so it's no big deal." From Michelle's relaxed manner, it seemed to Naomi that the information was not confidential. But was Naomi ever wrong!

One Sunday evening a couple of weeks later, Naomi was in Michelle's apartment watching television with Michelle and Lisa, another friend, when during a TV show, the TV mother sarcastically said to her son, "I'm sure a few visits to a thera-pist's office would straighten you out!" That comment jolted Naomi's memory so she asked, "Hey, Michelle, how's it going with your therapist?" Michelle instantly pursed her lips and shot Naomi a deadly look that clearly meant, "How could you ask me that now?" Lisa quickly turned to Michelle and in-quisitively asked, "Michelle, I didn't know you were in ther-apy. Why didn't you tell me?" Upset by Lisa's question, Michelle nervously responded, "There's really nothing to talk about." Naomi's heart sank because she knew right away she had unintentionally betrayed Michelle's confidence and em-barrassed her in front of Lisa. She hoped Michelle would forgive her.

Naomi ended up in this difficult situation because she wasn't aware that Michelle didn't want her to tell anyone that she was in therapy. Naomi and Michelle held different assumptions about the confidentiality of that information. Naomi assumed it wasn't confidential because Michelle hadn't explicitly said it was, and Michelle assumed that as a good friend, Naomi would have known without being told that the information was con-fidential. Clearly, their differing assumptions landed Naomi in hot water. Making the wrong assumption about confidential-ity is a communication blunder that can result in losing the trust of friends, family members or colleagues.

One evening, my friend Roger called to make plans with me. The last time we had spoken, about two weeks earlier, he told me that his sister Nancy had ended a serious seven-month relationship with a man because he had lied to her and said he was divorced when in fact his divorce was a long way from being final. In that conversation Roger had said that his sister was very upset about the whole thing and that he was spending a lot of time talking to her. I liked Roger's sister, so this time when he called, I asked him, "How's Nancy doing?" "Oh boy," Roger said, "funny you should ask. She and her boyfriend got back together, but now she isn't talking to me." "What?" I asked, confused. "Why isn't she talking to you?" "Well, apparently the breakup wasn't supposed to be public knowledge. She is furious with me for telling people about their breakup and especially about why they broke up—that her boyfriend didn't tell her the truth about his divorce." "How does she know you told other people about it?" I asked. "Because a mutual friend called to console her and told her I was the one who passed on the information about their breakup." "But, Roger, I don't understand how that happened. When Nancy first told you about the breakup, didn't she tell you to keep it confidential?" "No," he said, "she didn't say anything like that to me. So I assumed it was okay to tell other people. Besides, I figured my sister would be happy if I let people know that she was available to date again. Instead, my sister said that as her brother I should have known better and kept my mouth shut." "Did you apologize to her?" "Yes, but she's still angry with me. She said she doesn't want to talk to me because she can't trust me. She's afraid I might say something stupid again. There is really nothing I can do to make her change her mind. Sooner or later she'll get over it."

Roger made a communication blunder that created unnecessary conflict when he assumed that what his sister had told him was not confidential. He learned through this experience that what is private and confidential to one person may not be to another.

· · · · ·

COMMUNICATION BLUNDER

When someone tells you something personal, it is a blunder to decide on your own whether or not that information is confidential.

You can get into trouble not only when you open your mouth to reveal something that *should not* be revealed, but also when you do not reveal something that *should* be revealed. How? Just follow this next story and you will see what happens when you assume something *is* confidential and it isn't.

My friend Judy got into trouble when she tried to protect Patricia, her friend and colleague. Patricia was planning her wedding in New York City and was having trouble making a final decision about where to have it. She asked Judy, her maid of honor, "Would you mind doing me a favor? My fiancé and I have whittled down our options for a wedding location to three places and we don't know which one to pick. I'd really appreciate it if you would come with me this weekend to see the places and give me your opinion." Judy felt especially honored that her friend valued her taste and wanted her opinion, so she said she'd be happy to look at the wedding sites with her.

The Monday after their weekend wedding adventure, Judy was at work when Sarah casually asked her what she did over the weekend. "Actually I had a very interesting weekend," Judy said. "I visited wedding places with Patricia." "Really?"

Sarah said. "Which places did you visit?" Judy felt uncomfortable answering because she wasn't sure whether Patricia wanted to keep that information confidential. But she decided that telling Sarah the names of the places wasn't too personal, so she listed them. Then Sarah became even more curious. "Oh," she said, "I recently went to a wedding at the first place. It was very extravagant. Do you know how much that place and the other places cost per person?" Judy knew, but she assumed that Patricia wouldn't want anyone else to know, so she lied and said, "I don't know anything about the prices. Patricia didn't tell me." Judy was comfortable with her answer because she thought she had responded effectively and still maintained Patricia's confidence.

Later, however, Judy discovered that she had actually made a huge communication blunder by assuming that Patricia wanted her to keep the price information confidential. A few days later when she, Patricia and Sarah were talking about the wedding, Sarah asked Patricia, "Do you mind telling me what each of the places you looked at costs per person? I'm curious." Judy tensed up at the question, remembering how she had lied when Sarah asked her the very same question. Judy assumed that Patricia would also avoid answering, but to Judy's amazement, without any hesitation Patricia told Sarah how much each place cost. "Wow," Sarah said, "that's much more than I thought it would cost for a wedding." "I know," said Patricia, who continued, "Judy was also amazed by the prices when she heard them last weekend. But everything is so much more expensive in Manhattan." As Patricia finished her sentence, Sarah turned to Judy and spitefully said, "Judy, why did you tell me that you didn't know the prices when you did?"

There was nothing Judy could say to redeem herself. She was caught. Judy softly mumbled, "Sorry, I didn't think Patricia wanted anyone to know." In an attempt to keep the confidence of one friend, she chose to lie to another friend.

Judy made a communication blunder by not asking Patricia whether or not she should keep the prices confidential, and then lying to Sarah to cover up the information she knew.

When Judy and Patricia were visiting the wedding places, Judy assumed the information she learned that day was personal. She should have used a communication wonder and specifically asked Patricia, "Do you want me to keep the information about your wedding plans confidential?" Patricia would then have had the opportunity to say, "Yes, please keep it between us," or "No, it's not confidential. You can tell anyone anything they want to know."

Since Judy didn't ask Patricia about confidentiality and Sarah unexpectedly put her on the spot by asking about prices, Judy should have used the second part of the communication wonder. Instead of lying, Judy should have said sincerely, "I'm not sure if Patricia would want me to discuss the cost of the wedding with anyone. Would you mind asking her yourself?"

This communication wonder is extremely useful whenever someone shares personal information with you or you are asked to share that information. It is important to remember that every person maintains a different level of privacy in his or her life. It is unwise to assume that another person has the same sense of what is or is not confidential as you. Make it easy on yourself: Don't put yourself in the position of having to determine whether or not what someone told you is confidential.

COMMUNICATION WONDER

Keep It Private

1. When someone tells you something personal, ask, "Is this confidential information, to be kept between us?"

2. If you don't know whether something is confidential and someone asks you about it, say, "I'm not sure if he would want me to discuss that with anyone. Would you mind asking him yourself?"

Rule 31

· · · · · ·

Invite
with
Caution

YOU MAY HAVE NOTICED that when you are considerate toward others, you earn their appreciation and cooperation. So it naturally follows that it is in your best interests to be considerate toward others all the time. True, although this is definitely easier said than done. Why? Because we unknowingly let little acts of thoughtlessness creep into our daily routines at home and at work. Despite our best intentions, these little inconsiderate acts often offend others and persuade them to become uncooperative and antagonistic toward us. This chapter draws your attention to one of these small, inconsiderate acts that can create unnecessary conflict. It's a simple communication blunder that can happen when you extend an invitation. Although just a little blunder, it carries a big consequence. In the following stories you will learn about this common communication blunder so you can avoid it and the conflict that results from it.

Robin and her husband returned home from a two-week vacation in Europe. A couple of days later she called her friend Gail. "Hi, Gail. I'm back in New York. How are you?" she asked. "I'm fine," Gail replied. "How was your vacation?" "Oh, it was fantastic. We had such a good time. I can't wait to show you the pictures and tell you all about it." "I have some new things to tell you, too," Gail said. "So much has happened while you were gone. I can't wait to see you and tell you everything. When can we get together?" "How about Thursday night?" asked Robin, who continued, "It's the only night I'm free this week. I'm tied up next weekend with family things." Gail had plans on Thursday night, but she really wanted to share the exciting news that she was being considered for a promotion to partner at her law firm. She also wanted to hear more about Robin's trip. So Gail quickly decided to rearrange her Thursday night plans to make time for Robin. "Thursday night is fine," she told Robin. "I have other plans that night, but I'll change them. Want to meet for dinner?" "Good idea," Robin said. "I'll call you Thursday morning at work to set up the time and place." "Great. I'm looking forward to seeing you," Gail said.

On Thursday, Gail received the follow-up phone call from Robin as planned. "Hi," Robin said. "How about meeting for dinner tonight at seven-thirty at the Italian restaurant on the corner of East Fifty-fourth Street and Second Avenue?" "Sure," Gail replied, "that sounds good." "Okay," said Robin, who casually added, "By the way, I spoke to Jill the other day and I invited her to have dinner with us tonight." "Jill?" Gail repeated. "Yes, you know her. You met her at my cousin's party last month and you said you liked her." "Oh," Gail said, not sure what to say because from what she remembered, she hadn't particularly liked Jill, nor did she want to have dinner with her. But she thought, "What can I do about it now? How can I ask Robin to call Jill and uninvite her?" Not wanting to make a big deal out of the situation, Gail decided to let it go and said, "See you tonight."

That night at 7:30 Gail met up with Robin and Jill at the restaurant. Over dinner, they looked at Robin's vacation photos and Robin and Jill tied up the conversation, talking mostly about Robin's trip as well as Jill's new boyfriend. Gail wasn't interested in hearing about Jill's new boyfriend and she didn't feel comfortable sharing her news about the promotion with Robin in front of Jill, who was only an acquaintance. So Gail kept quiet for a good part of the evening. As they ate Gail became more and more annoyed with Robin for ruining her evening by inviting Jill to join them without asking her first. At last the dinner ended and Robin and Gail decided to share a cab home.

As soon as they sat down in the cab, Robin asked, "Gail, you were so quiet tonight. Is everything okay?" Gail almost replied, "Yes, everything's fine," to avoid making waves, but she couldn't hold her tongue anymore. She said, "Yes, something is wrong. I went out of my way to rearrange my plans for tonight so that we could spend time together and catch up on things, but you just went right ahead and invited Jill to join us for dinner without asking me. I didn't feel comfortable talking about my personal life with Jill there." "Oh," Robin said, surprised at such a sharp response from Gail. "I thought you liked Jill." "Well," Gail replied, "it doesn't matter whether I like her or not. I expected to spend time alone talking to you. If you had asked me whether I wanted you to invite her, I would have said no." Trying to defend her actions, Robin said, "I didn't mean to offend you. I haven't seen either of you in weeks, and I thought it would be nice if we all got together." "Well, it wasn't nice for me," Gail said. "I wasn't interested in talking to Jill and it didn't seem like you were interested in hearing about what is going on in my life." "I'm sorry," Robin said. "I never thought about it like that. Gail, you know that I really care about you. I didn't mean to hurt your feelings. I didn't think it through. In the future I'll be sure to ask you before I invite someone to join us." Gail was satisfied with Robin's apology because Robin had used the two-part apology. Robin made Gail realize that she understood what she did wrong and wouldn't make the same communication blunder again.

COMMUNICATION BLUNDER

When you have plans with someone, it is a blunder to take it upon yourself to invite an additional person(s) to join in on those plans.

In the next story you will see how this same small, inconsiderate act causes strife in a marriage. One Wednesday evening, Karen and Jerry, a married couple, decide to go out to dinner on Friday night. Usually, they reserve Friday nights for family dinners at home with their two teenage daughters. But because this was a hectic week at work for Karen, they agree it would be a good idea instead to go out for a casual dinner without their daughters on Friday. With their plans set, Karen tells Jerry, "I'm going to the supermarket for a few things and I'm going to buy something special for the girls for dinner on Friday while we're out. I'll be back in an hour."

After Karen leaves, Jerry begins opening the mail and the phone rings. "Hey," says Bill, Jerry's golf buddy. "I was just wondering whether you want to play on Saturday." "Sure," Jerry says. Bill responds, "I'll give you a call later this week with the tee-off time." "All right," says Jerry, who spontaneously adds, "By the way, Karen and I are going out to dinner Friday night. If you and your wife want to join us that would be great." "Sounds good to me," Bill says. "I don't think we have plans. Just let me check with my wife and I'll call you back later tonight." "Okay, let me know," Jerry says. They hang up and Jerry continues going through the mail.

When Karen returns from the supermarket, Jerry gets up to help her put the food away. "By the way," he says nonchalantly, "Bill called while you were out." "Uh-huh," Karen says, concentrating more on where she's putting the food than on what Jerry is saying. "I invited him and his wife to join us for dinner on Friday." Now that comment instantly captures Karen's attention. "What?" she says. "Why did you do that?" Jerry responds, "Well, we haven't been out with them in a long time, so I thought it would be nice." Karen immediately starts shaking her head, which is a sure sign to Jerry that he has done something wrong. He quickly interjects, "They may not come. Bill said he would check with his wife and call me back." Now that response completely infuriates Karen. "Jerry," she says, "okay, let me see if I have this right. Bill is checking with his wife?" "Yes," Jerry innocently replies. "Well then," Karen continues, "how is it that Bill knows to check with his wife before he gives you an answer and you didn't know to check with your wife before you ask someone to dinner?" Jerry has no response to that question.

"You know, I don't particularly enjoy their company," Karen says. "His wife is so critical of everyone and everything that I feel uncomfortable around her. I was planning to have a casual evening. I wanted to go to a hamburger place and wear sneakers and jeans." "So," says Jerry, "we can still go for burgers. What's the problem?" Karen forcefully responds, "I'll tell you what the problem is. Now, because you invited Bill and his picky wife, we'll have to make a dinner reservation somewhere and I'll have to get dressed up. Thanks to you, it's no longer a casual evening. You turned this whole thing into an event by asking them to come. Why did you do that?" "I'm sorry. I never thought that inviting them was such a big deal. You weren't home when he called, so I just asked him." "You knew I'd be home soon," Karen exclaims. "You should have waited to ask them because those plans involve me. It was just plain rude and inconsiderate of you. I don't invite people without asking you! Even Bill knew to talk to his wife before he made a decision." Jerry thinks Karen is overreacting.

Just then the phone rings and Jerry picks it up. "Hi, Jerry," Bill says. "I talked to my wife and we'd be happy to go to dinner with you Friday night." "Great," Jerry says, glancing apprehensively over at Karen, who is glaring at him. Jerry continues, "I'm kind of busy at the moment. Can we work out the details tomorrow?" "Sure," Bill says. "Why don't you give me a call?" "Okay, will do," Jerry says, and hangs up the phone and slowly turns to his wife. "They're coming," he says anxiously.

"Look, Jerry, you never should have asked them to come. I'm really angry with you for putting me in a situation like this, but there's nothing I can do about it now. You better promise me you'll never invite anyone to go out with us again unless you discuss it with me first." "Okay, I promise," Jerry quickly agrees, hoping to end this distressful conversation. The entire experience puts Karen in a bad mood. She'd rather stay home Friday night and have dinner with her daughters.

Jerry made a communication blunder when he invited Bill and his wife to dinner before getting his wife's approval. Jerry didn't mean to offend or upset his wife, but he wrongly assumed that Karen would be fine with their company because he was fine with it. His spontaneous invitation angered Karen and created unnecessary friction in their relationship.

If Jerry had known about the communication wonder he could have avoided the confrontation. The safest and surest way for Jerry to handle this situation would have been for him to ask his wife before inviting Bill and his wife to join them for dinner. If Jerry had done that, Karen would have felt that he cared about her and respected her opinion, which was, without question, that she didn't want to have dinner with Bill and his wife. What could have been a peaceful, pleasant evening turned out to be an unpleasant one, simply because of a few words that Jerry neglected to say to his wife.

It's usually more enjoyable to spend time with people you choose to be with than to spend time with people who are chosen for you to be with. Always seek approval from people with whom you have set plans *before* you invite anyone else to join in on those plans. This communication wonder encourages you to make one little, considerate comment that will mean a lot to others.

COMMUNICATION WONDER

Invite with Caution

If you have plans with someone, seek
that person's approval before you invite
anyone else to join in on those plans.

Rule 32

· · · · ·

Have Balanced Conversations

IT'S NOT HARD TO identify self-absorbed people because they always talk about themselves and what's going on in their life. A self-absorbed person doesn't stop to ask you how you're doing. It's as if he is on a stage reciting a monologue and you happen to be his audience. He talks at you, not with you. You quickly lose interest in the conversation and look for a way to escape. Why do you feel this way? Simply because you are involved in an unbalanced, one-sided conversation in which one person does most of the talking while the other person does most of the listening.

Our words reveal the kind of person we are, so it is important to pay attention to what we say and the impression we create with our words. When we engage in unbalanced conversations we persuade others to stop listening to us and dislike us.

I draw your attention to unbalanced conversations because
many times, without realizing it, we turn ourselves into that
self-centered person by unintentionally taking over a conversation. For example, a woman might start talking and expect
the other person to interrupt her when he has something to
say. However, the other person might just nod his head patiently, say "uh-huh" and wait for her to stop talking because
he is uncomfortable interrupting her. At other times, someone
might unknowingly monopolize a conversation simply because
he gets caught up in what he's saying and doesn't realize that
he hasn't given the other person a chance to talk. In situations
like this, other people may view the talker as self-absorbed
and inconsiderate.

It is important to think about how we conduct ourselves in
conversations. With a communication wonder we can avoid
creating unbalanced conversations and instead engage in
conversations that encourage people to talk to us, listen to us
and enjoy our company.

This first story is an extreme example of an unbalanced conversation. I had this conversation as a student at law school
when I was interviewing for a summer job at a law firm. Every
year the summer job recruitment process was the same. Employers would visit the campus to conduct standard twenty-
minute job interviews with law students. After the first round of
interviews, employers would select students for a second round
of job interviews to be held at their law firm. My first round interview with Mr. Gladstone stands out vividly in my memory.

When I walked into the interview room Mr. Gladstone and

I shook hands and introduced ourselves. As we sat down he said, "Laurie, I've seen your résumé, now tell me what area of law you like and why." I was well prepared and eager to talk about my interest in litigation and why it was right for me. But as soon as I said, "I'm interested in litigation . . ." Mr. Gladstone quickly jumped in to say, "As a matter of fact, I was recently appointed to head the litigation department." He went on to tell me about his position and his background. I didn't like being interrupted, but I sat there patiently and politely listening to him, nodding my head and occasionally smiling as I waited for my turn to speak. He continued talking, mostly about himself, until finally he paused for a moment and asked me a question about law school. I answered and then asked him whether the associates in litigation work with lawyers in other departments to gain experience in other areas of law. "Well," he said, "at this firm there is a lot of crossover among departments." Then he went on to share with me, in full detail, how in the past he had spent time working with lawyers from the real estate group, the intellectual property group and even the tax group.

When he finished his five-minute monologue, I expected him to ask me more questions that would give me a chance to tell him something about myself, especially since we were more than halfway through the interview. I thought, "Doesn't he want to learn something about me since I'm the one being interviewed?" To my disappointment, he still didn't involve me in the conversation. Instead, he told me about a particular case he was working on that he found very challenging. I was frustrated at not being given a chance to talk. I didn't like Mr. Gladstone. The more he talked about himself and his interests, the more I lost interest in him and the firm he represented. When Mr. Gladstone finished talking, he looked down at his watch and said, "Wow, this interview went quickly. I'm sorry, but our time is up." I wasn't sorry.

We shook hands and I said, "Thank you for your time." I was convinced that Mr. Gladstone was not going to hire me because he never took the time to ask me any questions that would have indicated he was interested in me. So when he said, "Laurie, it was a pleasure meeting you and I want you to know that I have already decided to invite you to our New York office for a second-round interview," I was shocked. I walked out of the room trying to figure out what had just happened. I wondered, "How could this man have enjoyed meeting me when he hardly spent any time getting to know me?"

After giving the situation some thought, I realized that Mr. Gladstone liked me because I patiently and politely listened to him toot his own horn. Although it's true that I got what I wanted—an offer to come to New York—Mr. Gladstone didn't get what he wanted—a second interview with me—because he made a communication blunder. Mr. Gladstone's unbalanced conversation instantly persuaded me to dislike him, and since he represented the firm, I chose not to take him up on his offer. I couldn't imagine working at a firm with this self-centered man as the head of the litigation department.

> ### COMMUNICATION BLUNDER
>
> It is a blunder to create an unbalanced conversation.

You might think that you would never act like Mr. Gladstone because his self-centeredness was so apparent and extreme. But unbalanced conversations are very common. They occur between friends, family members and colleagues every day. In the next story, you will observe what happens when Nancy controls an entire conversation that prevents Veronica, her colleague, from telling her about something that is important to her.

It's 12:30 P.M. on a Monday, and Nancy and Veronica, who are coworkers, walk across the street to have lunch at a café. They don't see each other much because they work on different floors for different bosses, so they arrange to have lunch together periodically. Veronica is happy to get out of the office for a little while because she can't stand being around her boss anymore. He's a perfectionist and is seldom satisfied with her work. That morning he went so far as to embarrass her by criticizing her in front of other people for arriving fifteen minutes late, even though she had a good reason for it. After putting up with him for a year, Veronica thinks it might be time to quit and start looking for a new job. She would prefer to work things out with her boss because she hates the thought of job hunting, but at this point, she doesn't see any other way out. Veronica wants to get Nancy's advice on what she should do since Nancy has been working at this company for many years.

Once they sit down at a table and unwrap their sandwiches, Veronica asks, "Nancy, how was your weekend?" "Wonderful! My husband and the kids and I took the train from New York City to Philadelphia to visit my parents." Veronica likes Nancy and is interested in hearing more about her weekend trip, so she asks, "Did you stay overnight?" "Yes. We stayed over Friday and Saturday night. My parents just love having us visit. They really enjoy spending time with my kids, and of course my kids love the attention they get from their grandparents. All this works out so well for Joe and me because we were able to go out alone Saturday night while my parents baby-sat. We had such a good time. I miss spending time with my mom and dad, but they're coming to New York to visit us in a couple weeks." "Oh, that's nice," says Veronica, who is now waiting for Nancy to stop talking so she can shift the conversation to her problem with her boss. But Nancy doesn't leave an opening for Veronica. As Nancy continues talking, Veronica repeatedly says "uh-huh," barely listening to what Nancy says. As time passes, Veronica gets more and more annoyed with Nancy for monopolizing the conversation. Veronica thinks, "We've almost finished eating lunch and Nancy hasn't asked me anything about my weekend or anything else."

Finally, Veronica interrupts Nancy and says, "I'm sorry to interrupt, but I really want to talk to you about something." "Oh, okay," Nancy responds, startled by the interruption, "but I really don't have much time left to talk. I want to get back to the office early to make up for the time I lost on Friday when I left early." Veronica doesn't like being rushed, but she really wants Nancy's advice, so she starts to tell her about her problem with her boss and what happened that morning.

As Veronica speaks, Nancy looks at her watch and begins to gather up the garbage on the table. Then she says, "Veronica, I'm sorry but I don't have any more time. Let's meet for lunch tomorrow so we can talk about your problem then." "Yeah, sure," answers Veronica, who at this point is so agitated by Nancy that she can't even think about seeing her for lunch the next day. They get up from the table, throw out their garbage and head back to the office. Nancy feels refreshed and happy as she walks back into the office building. She enjoyed having lunch with Veronica and talking about her weekend in Philadelphia. Veronica, on the other hand, walks back to the office feeling frustrated and angry with Nancy for rudely monopolizing the entire conversation.

Nancy made a communication blunder when she did all the talking and none of the listening. Nancy did not intentionally ignore her friend, she merely got carried away talking about her family. She assumed that Veronica wanted to hear what she had to say or she would have interrupted her sooner. But from Veronica's perspective, Nancy was self-centered and had no interest in listening to anyone talk but herself.

Nancy should have used a communication wonder to turn her one-sided conversation into a balanced conversation. She should have asked Veronica a question to give her the opportunity to talk about what was important to her. By talking and sharing their thoughts equally, Nancy and Veronica would have had the chance to confide in each other and show interest in each other. When a conversation is balanced and both people share a comparable amount of time talking and listening, both people feel heard and satisfied.

It's important to remember that the words you choose to say or not say to someone have the power to persuade that person to listen to or ignore you. From now on, when you're involved in a conversation, check yourself periodically to see if you're talking too much. If you are, then immediately use this communication wonder to regain balance in your conversation so that people enjoy talking to you.

COMMUNICATION WONDER

Have Balanced Conversations

If you find yourself talking too much, regain balance
in your conversation by asking the other person
a question and listening to his answer.

Rule 33

• • • • •

Say What You Mean

"I CAN'T BELIEVE YOU did that! You should know me well enough by now to understand that what I said was not what I meant!" Now that's a statement you might have made to someone who misinterpreted what you said and then didn't do what you wanted him to do. You think to yourself, "Why do I have to spell everything out for him? What I meant was so obvious." Defending his position, he responds, "How was I supposed to know what you meant when you didn't say it? I asked you a question and I heard your answer. I'm not a mind reader!" Frustrated, you reply, "You should know better than to take every word I say at face value. You don't have to be a mind reader, you just need a little common sense."

How do we end up in situations like this? At times, when someone asks us a question about something that affects us, we may feel uncomfortable saying what we mean because we don't want to appear unfriendly or difficult. Yet we expect the other person to read between the lines to know exactly what we're thinking. Then, when that person doesn't read between the lines as we expected him to, and we don't get what we want, we become disappointed and angry and blame him for the problem that we created. Does this make sense? Is there ever a time in a relationship when the other person automatically knows what we mean, even when we don't explicitly say it? Probably not. So to eliminate the risk of being misunderstood and to give ourselves the best shot at getting what we want, we must focus on saying what we mean and meaning what we say. The stories you are about to read demonstrate how easy it is to unintentionally set yourself up to be misunderstood, disappointed and hurt when you don't say what you mean. When you say to someone, "Do whatever you want," you will probably end up with what you don't want. There is a simple communication wonder that reminds you of the importance of saying what's on your mind to encourage people to cooperate with you and give you what you want.

Let me give you a perfect example of how my friend Alison set herself up to be hurt and disappointed by her husband, Rob, because she didn't say what she meant. Alison and Rob live in Los Angeles and have been married for three years. Every year they celebrate Valentine's Day together with a romantic dinner and an exchange of presents. It was February, and as usual Alison was looking forward to Valentine's Day. "Rob," she asked, "where do you want to have dinner this year on Valentine's Day?" "I have a restaurant in mind," Rob said with a smile. "I know you love surprises. I've already made the reservation and I'm not telling you where we're going." "Sounds great to me," Alison said. She liked surprises and loved Valentine's Day even more because it was the one day that she could be assured of a meaningful, romantic evening with her husband.

But Alison's excitement quickly dulled when Rob asked her, "Alison, do you really want to exchange presents again this year? Remember last year when we both spent so much time trying to find each other the perfect gift and then in the end, we both returned the gifts anyway? It seemed like such a waste of time. I think we should skip the whole gift thing this year. What do you think?" Alison was hurt that Rob didn't want to get her a present because it always made Valentine's Day special, even if she did have to exchange her present for something else. But she didn't want to force Rob to get her a present if he didn't want to, so she reluctantly said, "Well, a present would be nice, but I suppose we don't have to exchange presents again this year if you don't want to." Alison hoped that Rob would hear her comment, read between the lines and respond with something like, "It sounds to me like you still like the present idea, so let's do it again this year." Unfortunately Rob didn't say anything like that and Alison became upset and disappointed when he said, "Okay, so we're agreed. No presents this year. Just a nice romantic dinner."

By the time Valentine's Day arrived Alison was no longer upset with Rob for not wanting to buy her a present. She had convinced herself that Rob knew she wanted a present and was tricking her into thinking she wasn't getting one to enhance the surprise when he gave her one. Alison had bought Rob a pocket camera and planned to give Rob his present after he gave her the present she expected from him. But their romantic dinner date came and went. They had a fantastic meal at a romantic Italian restaurant in Santa Monica, but Alison never received the present she had anticipated from Rob and she was extremely hurt and disappointed. She knew it was too late to do anything about it so she decided to keep her disappointment to herself.

At home, Alison and Rob changed into comfortable clothes and headed into the den to watch TV. Rob noticed that Alison was unusually quiet. He couldn't imagine why because they had just enjoyed a wonderful evening together. So he asked her, "Alison, is something wrong? You're so quiet." Alison's disappointment quickly turned to anger when she realized he had no idea that he had hurt her feelings.

She looked him straight in the eye and said coldly, "You don't have a clue why I'm so quiet, do you? Well, I'll tell you why. I'm very upset. For the past three years and even before we were married we've always given each other presents on Valentine's Day, and now, suddenly, this year it's not important to you. Maybe that's because I'm not important to you. I bought you a present again this year. Do you know why? Because you're important to me." Rob was totally confused by his wife's sudden burst of emotion. "What are you talking about? You bought me a present? Why? We agreed not to exchange presents this year." "No," Alison answered. "I didn't agree. Maybe if you'd listened to what I said, you'd have known that." Now Rob was completely frustrated and upset. "I don't remember exactly what you said, but whatever it was, it sure sounded to me like you wanted to do the very same thing I wanted to do," he responded loudly. "How should I have known that when you said you agreed, you really didn't agree?" Alison rolled her eyes and responded, "Oh, come on, Rob, don't give me that. Of course I wanted a present for Valentine's Day! Every woman does. I shouldn't have to tell you that." Rob got up and muttered, "Well, I suppose you do have to tell me," and he stomped into the bedroom to escape Alison's reprimand.

Alison and Rob ended up in an argument that didn't have to happen. Rob didn't get Alison a present, not because she wasn't important to him, not because he chose to ignore her wishes, not because he was a jerk, but simply because he took her words at face value. Alison knew all along that she wanted a present from Rob, but she didn't say that to him. Instead, she halfheartedly agreed with him and set herself up to be disappointed and hurt. Alison made a communication blunder when she expected Rob to read her mind and know that she wanted a present.

> **COMMUNICATION BLUNDER**
>
> It is a blunder to expect someone
> to read your mind.

Unfortunately, in this next story, Ashley also set herself up for disappointment when she didn't say what she meant in her response to a question from a friend. It happened when Ashley decided to throw a surprise birthday party for Crystal, her best friend and roommate. She invited ten of their friends to dinner in a small private room she reserved at a Mexican restaurant in Manhattan. The dinner party was going to cost

Ashley a little more than she originally planned because she decided to include wine with dinner. But the additional expense was worth it because she wanted the night to be special for her friend. Two days before the birthday party, Ashley received a telephone call from her friend Wendy, who was invited to the party. "Hi, Ashley," Wendy said. "It's so nice of you to throw a surprise party for Crystal. I'm really looking forward to it. But I have a question for you." "Sure," Ashley said. "What is it?" "I was wondering if I could bring a friend to the party who will be visiting me this weekend." Ashley was stunned by Wendy's question. She didn't want a total stranger to come to the party, which was already costing her more than she expected. She also felt that Wendy had a lot of nerve imposing on her in this way. Yet in spite of all this, Ashley found it impossible to get the word no out of her mouth.

Unable to say no directly, Ashley chose an indirect way of getting her point across. "Wendy, I don't think your friend would have a good time at the party because she won't know anyone there." "That won't be a problem for her," Wendy said confidently. "My friend is very outgoing. She gets along with everyone." "Really?" Ashley said. "But there's something else. I already gave the restaurant the final count on the number of people coming so everything is already set." "Oh," Wendy said. "I'd be happy to call the restaurant for you to let them know there'll be one more person." Ashley didn't know what else to say. She had pretty much told Wendy not to bring her friend to the party, but nothing registered with Wendy. Ashley was upset with Wendy for being rude and deliberately ignoring all her hints that were intended to mean, "Don't bring your friend to the party." Seeing no way out, Ashley resigned herself to the situation and said, "I guess she can come. I'll call the restaurant." "Great," Wendy said. "I know you'll like my friend when you meet her." Ashley couldn't care less about Wendy's friend. All she cared about at that moment was how much she disliked Wendy for selfishly imposing on her and making her spend more money on a person she didn't know. Ashley was angry with herself for not saying exactly what she meant. She didn't want Wendy's friend to come to dinner, and at that point she hoped Wendy wouldn't come either.

What Ashley didn't realize was that she made a communication blunder when she didn't say what she meant. Although Wendy put Ashley in an uncomfortable situation by asking if she could bring a friend to the party, Ashley managed the situation poorly. Ashley expected Wendy to read her mind, but no matter how many hints she gave her, Wendy never understood that her weekend guest wasn't welcome at the party.

If Ashley had said what she meant in no uncertain terms, something like, "Wendy, I'm sorry but your friend can't come. I planned a small party and I only want Lisa's closest friends there," there would have been no room for misinterpretation. Although Wendy would not have liked that answer to her question, she would have had to accept it. By saying what she meant, Ashley wouldn't have resented Wendy for taking advantage of her.

What is the lesson here? It's simple. Just understand and accept the fact that people, even close friends, will take your words at face value, so it is important to answer truthfully and say what you mean. If you don't say what you want, you probably won't get it. Before responding to a question, such as Rob's question to Alison about Valentine's Day presents or Wendy's question to Ashley about bringing her friend to the party, use a communication wonder and ask yourself, "Am I about to say what I mean and mean what I say?" If your answer is no, then beware. You are setting yourself up to be misunderstood, hurt and disappointed. If your answer is yes and you are about to say what you mean, then congratulations. You have wisely set yourself up to be understood so you get what you want with the cooperation of the people around you.

COMMUNICATION WONDER

Say What You Mean

When someone asks you a question about something that personally affects you, be sure to say what you mean, or you risk being disappointed.

Rule 34

· · · · ·

Avoid After-the-Fact Comments

YOU WOULDN'T WANT TO disrespect someone by using belittling words, would you? You wouldn't want to insult someone you care about, would you? Well, chances are, in spite of good intentions you have probably inadvertently said the wrong thing at the wrong time and upset someone you care about. In this chapter you will learn how to determine if you're saying something wrong so that your words won't work against you to create bad feelings. In the following stories you will see how well-intentioned people offend others by picking the wrong time to say something. You will also learn a communication wonder to help you choose your timing wisely so that what you say has a positive impact on your relationships.

My friend Jill was so bothered by a comment made to her by another friend that she remembered to tell me about it a week later when she called me. Jill and Steve are a married couple who live in New York City and are moving to the suburbs very shortly. They spent many months house hunting on Long Island every weekend before finding their dream house. The price was more than they wanted to pay, but they decided it was worth it because the house has four bedrooms, three bathrooms, a new kitchen and a big family room that opens onto a large backyard. It is close enough to Manhattan so they will be able to comfortably commute to and from work on the Long Island Rail Road. Coincidentally, the house is just twenty-five minutes from Jill's college friend Pam, who lives in the nearby town of Great Neck. Pam moved to Great Neck with her husband and son about a year earlier. Since her move, Pam and Jill haven't seen much of each other, but they plan to spend more time together once Jill moves to Long Island.

Jill began her story by telling me that two days after she and Steve closed on their new house, she eagerly called Pam to tell her the exciting news. Unfortunately, Pam didn't respond quite the way Jill expected her to. "Congratulations," Pam said. "So you bought a house close to Great Neck? I can hardly believe it." "Yes, it took us forever to make a final decision. There were so many considerations, but this house has all the features Steve and I wanted," Jill answered. "Like what?" Pam asked. Jill went on to describe the great things about the house and then added, "But most important, it's close enough to the city so we can commute to and from work without much of a problem." "That's true," Pam said, "but did you check out the public school system in that town? I know you don't have kids now, but eventually you will and they'll be attending the schools there. Before I moved, I researched and compared the ratings of all the school districts on Long Island. The schools in the district where you bought your house rank on the lower end of the educational scale because they are poorly funded. If I remember correctly, the graduation rate in that area is lower than in many of the other Long Island districts. Did you know that?" As Jill listened to Pam share this "information," she felt as though Pam was intentionally trying to upset her. Jill responded by telling Pam, "I kind of knew that about the school district, but we don't have any kids right now and the house is so fantastic that Steve and I couldn't pass it up. Besides, I don't really need you to tell me that the schools are bad there. We already own the house. What's done is done."

Pam must have heard Jill's harsh tone because she changed the subject. But Jill would never forget Pam's comment and how her so-called friend upset her by putting her down and implying that she had made a bad decision about the house. At the time Jill wondered, "What kind of friend is Pam? Is she trying to pull a one-upmanship by showing me that her house is better than mine?" After her conversation with Pam, Jill knew that once she moved to Long Island, she wasn't going to be in a rush to invite Pam over.

Pam's comment was an indirect attack on Jill that left her feeling hurt and resentful. Did Pam know she was raining on Jill's parade? Probably not. She thought she was being helpful by informing Jill about the school district. People who give unintentional putdowns are rarely aware of what they're doing, but the people who receive them assume that it's intentional and seldom forget it. If Pam had shared the information with Jill *before* she purchased her house, it might have been helpful. Pam's communication blunder was that she shared the negative information *after* Jill had purchased her house. Pam's after-the-fact comment to Jill was pointless and harmful because there was nothing Jill could do to change the situation.

> ## COMMUNICATION BLUNDER
>
> It is a blunder to offer negative after-the-fact information about a person's choice when the decision cannot be changed.

The next story is another example of how an after-the-fact comment causes negative repercussions. One Thursday evening I was at a restaurant having dinner with two friends, Ryan, who works in finance, and Mark, who designs and sells customized computer software. We hadn't seen one another in a couple months so we decided to have dinner together to catch up on the happenings in our lives. During dinner I mentioned that I was going to shop for a new television that weekend. Ryan responded by telling us that he had bought an entertainment center a few months ago that included a large-screen TV, a VCR and a stereo with surround sound. "That sounds great," I said. "What kind of TV did you get?" "It's a thirty-six-inch Sharp flat screen. It has excellent picture quality. You might want to check it out and get the same one. You know what? After we finish dinner, why don't you both come back to my apartment and take a look at the entertainment center. Neither of you has been over in a long time and we're so close to my apartment. We can walk from here." "That's a good idea," I said. "Buying a TV these days is so complicated. There are so many choices. Maybe seeing yours will help me decide what to buy."

Mark also agreed to go to Ryan's apartment. "I'd like to see your new entertainment center," he said. But that wasn't all Mark said because he had a need to share some of his knowledge about technology. Although Mark was well informed on the latest technological advances because it helped him design better computer software for his clients, his "helpful" information at that time was not welcome. "Did you say you bought a VCR?" he asked. "That's right," Ryan said. "Well," Mark replied, "if you had asked me, I would have told you to forget about a VCR and buy a DVD player instead. The DVD technology provides better sound and pictures. In fact, I just bought a DVD player myself and it's ten times better than a VCR. Did you know that many of the new movies can't be played on a VCR anymore? You won't be able to rent them. At the very least you should have gotten a DVD/VCR combination player."

To Mark's surprise, Ryan was insulted and instantly became defensive. "Mark, what's the point of telling me that I should have gotten a DVD player? I just told you that I already bought a VCR and I'm happy with it. It's not very nice of you to sit there and tell me that I made the wrong choice." Mark seemed confused by Ryan's sudden change in mood. "You're reading into my comment. I didn't mean to offend you. I was just trying to be helpful by giving you some useful information." "Helpful? It's not helpful when you're telling me that I bought the wrong thing, especially when you know there's not a darn thing I can do about it now." Mark had no response to Ryan's comment so all of us just sat there in silence for a moment until I asked Ryan how his sister liked her new job. Mark seemed relieved when we started talking about something else. The rest of the conversation continued as if nothing unusual had happened.

But it was clear to me that something unusual had happened. When Mark got up to use the restroom at the end of the meal I nonchalantly asked Ryan if he still wanted us to come over to see his new entertainment center. "Actually, I'm not really up for having Mark come over anymore. He'll probably see my TV and tell me I should have gotten a different one. It's late and I'm tired anyway. Why don't you come over another time? Do you want me to call you tomorrow to tell you the exact model of my TV so you can look for it in the stores?" "Yes," I said, "I'd really appreciate that."

When Mark came back to the table Ryan told him that it was late and he was tired so he'd rather go home and get a good night's sleep instead of having us come over. Mark seemed fine with the change of plans, having no idea that the change was due to his unintentional putdown.

When we left the restaurant I thought about how ironic it was that Mark truly believed he was being helpful by telling Ryan that he should have bought a DVD player instead of the VCR that was already sitting in his apartment. Giving Ryan this information after he bought the system was clearly a communication blunder. I couldn't help but wonder whether Mark upset his customers the same way he upset Ryan by telling them they should have purchased a different computer that would have worked better with his software programs. It was unfortunate that Mark didn't understand that sharing negative information after the fact is a communication blunder because it comes off as a putdown that upsets people regardless of the well intended purpose.

What should Mark have said? He should have abided by the idea that "what's done is done." When something is complete and final and there is no way it can be changed, there is no point in offering someone additional information that is negative about his decision or purchase. Once it's after the fact, any contrary information is hurtful, harmful and unhelpful. Instead of telling Ryan that he made a mistake because a DVD player would have been a better purchase, Mark should have said nothing, or, "That's nice that you bought all that new entertainment equipment. I hope you enjoy it." The important thing to remember is that negative information can be valuable *before* a final decision is made, but once it's after the fact, keep it to yourself. However, it's fine to relay positive information at any time.

COMMUNICATION WONDER

Avoid After-the-Fact Comments

If someone's choice is final and unalterable, do not offer information that tells him something negative about his choice. Instead say nothing or something positive such as, "That's nice, enjoy it."

Rule 35

· · · · ·

Pay
with
Words

DO YOU KNOW the saying "Money talks"? It means that money sends a message. Money has the power to influence people, but money isn't the only thing with power. Your words also have power. They have the power to influence people to like, listen to, cooperate with and respect you so that you get what you want. When you learn to pay people with words of appreciation every day in little ways you show them that they are worth your attention. Your words make them feel valued in a way that money cannot. In turn, people will go out of their way to satisfy you because you appreciate their time and effort. Even when people earn a salary, it is often their desire for recognition and appreciation from colleagues and clients that motivates them to move beyond ordinary to reach extraordinary in the workplace. In the following stories you will discover new opportunities to pay people with sincere words of appreciation so that you can bring out the best in yourself and others as you achieve the results you want.

One Monday morning in April, when I was working at a nonprofit organization in Boston, I walked into my boss's office to discuss a project. Over the past months we had developed a friendly working relationship, so before we began discussing the project, my boss casually asked, "Laurie, how was your weekend? Did you do anything special?" "Yes," I told him, "I spent the weekend in New York at my parents' house. With the weather so nice we invited some people over for a backyard barbecue. There's nothing like an outdoor barbecue with friends and family on a beautiful sunny day. How was your weekend?" I asked. "Pretty good," he said. "I played golf on Saturday and came home just in time to meet the new gardeners I hired a couple weeks ago. They came to do the spring cleanup and I had told them exactly what I wanted them to do. I was shocked at the end of the day to see they had actually done everything I asked, so I didn't have to go outside and complain. My backyard looks so good now that I might have to have a party just to show it off!" I smiled at that comment, but something he had said stuck out in my mind. I didn't understand why he was surprised that his gardeners had done a good job, so I asked him, "Why were you so shocked that your new gardeners would follow your directions?" "Because," he said, "the gardeners I had last year never did anything right. That's why I fired them. Even when I specifically told them what to do, they'd follow my directions as long as I was watching them, but as soon as I went back in the house they'd go right back to being careless and lazy. Every week like clockwork I had to go outside to talk to them and complain about something. Either it was the dead leaves they'd blow into the bushes or the sprinkler heads they would run over and break with their lawn mowers. I wasted so much time and energy watching over them, just to get them to do the job I hired them to do." "That must have been annoying," I said. "You better believe it was! I hope these new guys work out. I'm so sick of looking for new gardeners every year."

Knowing my boss's tendency to be generous with criticism and stingy with words of appreciation, I wondered whether he had said anything nice to his new gardeners. I asked, "I'm just curious, did you tell the new gardeners that they did a good job and thank them for it?" "Thank them?" my boss repeated with a look of confusion. "Why should I thank them for doing their job? That's what I pay them to do. It's their responsibility to do a good job if they want to work for me. Anyway, I didn't see them when they left. I couldn't have thanked them even if I wanted to." "Oh," I said, somewhat startled by his very revealing answer. I wanted to respond by saying, "I'll bet you would have been able to find the gardeners before they left if they hadn't done a good job," but he was my boss so I kept my thoughts to myself and shifted the conversation to the project we were working on.

When I walked out of my boss's office I understood why he was stingy with his words of appreciation toward everyone at the office. He simply didn't think it was necessary for people to be paid with words of appreciation when they were already

being paid with money for the work they were doing. He figured that the fear of being fired is what should keep people in
line and working hard. My boss didn't realize that everyone
likes to hear words of praise when they do something well. He
made a communication blunder when he missed the opportunity to pay his gardeners with words of appreciation that
would have made them feel proud of their work and motivated them to work hard to please him the next time.

COMMUNICATION BLUNDER

It is a blunder to be stingy with
your words of appreciation.

In this next story I share a personal experience that will
show you how the power of words of appreciation can
instantly persuade someone to be kind and helpful to
you. A few years ago I wanted to set up a website—
www.lauriepuhn.com. At the time, I didn't know anything
about creating a website, but I made the bold decision to
jump in and try to do it anyway. When I hit a snag I called the
technical helpline for the website service. I waited on the
phone for twenty minutes listening to unpleasant elevator
music until I finally heard a friendly voice at the other end of
the line. "What can I do for you today?" she asked. "I have
two problems," I explained. "First, I tried to set up an e-mail
account from my website, but it isn't working. Can you tell
me if my website has the capacity for e-mail?" "It should," she

answered. "Maybe you inputted incorrect information. Let me see if I can figure out what you did and then we'll test it." Within five minutes, she had my e-mail working and even sent me an e-mail to demonstrate. "Okay," I said without delay, "now here's my second problem. I can't figure out how to post a photo on the website." "This is what you do," she said and then proceeded to tell me, step by step. Although I carefully followed her instructions, after fifteen minutes we still couldn't get the photo posted. She said that something was wrong with the system and I was going to require "advanced assistance." She told me she would put my request in the "advanced assistance" pile and I would have to wait for additional help. Totally frustrated by this time, I asked her, "You mean that after all this time I still have to wait?" She answered calmly, "Yes, you'll have to wait until nine A.M. tomorrow, when the advanced assistance people come back on duty. They'll give you a call. Have a nice day and I hope your website problem is solved."

Seconds later, after hearing the click of the phone, I knew I had made a communication blunder. This woman had spent twenty minutes patiently working with me, but I didn't bother to say thank you because I was frustrated by the experience. But then I thought to myself, "I bet this woman rarely gets recognition from the people she helps. Everyone who calls her must be frustrated because they only call her when they have technical problems." I was sorry that I had acted like one of the many people who just expect others to help them without showing any appreciation.

Suddenly I remembered the test e-mail she had sent me. So I went back to my e-mail account on the computer, pulled it up and wrote her a short thank-you e-mail. I wrote: "Hello. I just want to thank you for helping me with my website, www.lauriepuhn.com. I really appreciate your time and effort. You were incredibly patient! Have a nice day." A little later I received a reply: "You're very welcome. Your request is in for advanced assistance. Tomorrow morning I will talk to the supervisor in that department to be sure that your request is at the top of the list. You should receive a phone call from someone in advanced assistance by 10 A.M. tomorrow. If you don't, let me know and I'll check on it again for you."

Amazingly, as the technician had said, at nine the next morning I received a phone call from someone who was able to help me post my photo. My website was up and running. Of course I sent an e-mail to the woman I had spoken to the day before to let her know that my website was fixed and to thank her again. I believe the reason she made that extra effort to help me and check on the status of my request was because I had paid her generously with kind words of appreciation for what she had done. Once she knew that I valued her time and effort, she paid more attention to my problem and was willing to work harder to help me.

Anytime you express words of appreciation to someone for something he did, you will be giving him something more than money can buy. When you pay with words, you will find that the person will want to pay you back with his time and effort. Without spending a dime, you can spread an infinite amount of joy and happiness to those around you.

•   •   •   •   •

COMMUNICATION WONDER

Pay with Words

Money can't buy happiness, but your words can.
Be generous with your words of appreciation.

Epilogue

· · · · ·

Results Beyond Belief

HOW MANY PEOPLE do you speak to in a single day? A month? A year? The number is probably more than you could count. You go through your days talking to many different people at home, at work and in your social life. Yet until now you may not have realized the power of your words.

For a multitude of reasons, it is difficult to perceive or assess the impact that our words have on other people during the course of a conversation. When something doesn't go our way, we have a natural tendency to relinquish responsibility for the outcome and blame it on an unexpected circumstance, bad luck or even the shortcomings of another person.

But now, after reading the enlightening stories that reveal the Instant Persuasion blunders and wonders, you can see the direct link between what you say and the response you get. By using the Instant Persuasion rules in your daily conversations you will acquire more control over the responses you get from your friends, family members and colleagues.

With your new awareness and ability to say the right thing, at the right time, to the right person, you can instantly persuade people to like you, listen to you, cooperate with and respect you.

You can tap into your power of persuasion to reduce conflict, strengthen your relationships and add joy to your life and the lives of others.

Greater tact, skill and confidence will enable you to stand out from the crowd and be a role model for others.

Empowered with the Instant Persuasion rules, you will win people over in small ways every day so they are motivated to help you get what you want: a new job, a date, a favor, a stronger marriage, a lasting friendship, a promotion, as well as other things you desire. It takes only small changes in your words to create big changes in your life.

Expect to see those changes as soon as you start using the Instant Persuasion rules.

Expect to feel braver, wiser and more self-assured.

Expect to feel energized and inspired once you observe how quickly the rules work to connect you to people and give you the things you need, want and dream about.

From rule to rule in this book, I embrace a clear message: a vision of self-empowerment, a way to speak persuasively with honesty and integrity, a method that gives you control over your words to enable you to get the results you want by bringing out the best in yourself and others.

I have taken you on a journey of discovery intended to help you identify and reinforce the many communication wonders that will work for you, as well as the blunders that work against you.

Instant Persuasion is your handbook to winning people over, building trust and getting what you want. It's a practical guide to learning how to be your own best asset. It's your path to an astonishing personal transformation—one that only you can create, control and sustain to give you the personal satisfaction that you deserve.

I encourage you to change your mind-set to see communication in a new way. Over the years many of us have learned to pay close attention to what goes *into* our mouth: the foods we eat, the number of calories we ingest. Now with Instant Persuasion, it's time to broaden our focus to include what comes *out* of our mouth: the words we say and how they work to positively or negatively influence the quality of our relationships and the level of success we experience in our personal and professional life.

I hope *Instant Persuasion* has sparked your enthusiasm and belief in the power of words. You can get everything you want by giving people what they want—sincere words of recognition and a true sense of being valued *by you!* For many of us, our persuasive power is a valuable, untapped resource that lies dormant within us. Don't let it go to waste.

Grasp it.

Harness it.

Share it with others.

And expect to experience the thrill of success and happiness for a lifetime!

About the Author

LAURIE PUHN, J.D., president of Laurie Puhn Communications and founder of the Laurie Puhn Institute, is a graduate of Harvard College and Harvard Law School. She is an attorney, author, professional mediator, and dynamic public speaker. Puhn served on the board of the Harvard Mediation Program and trained Harvard Law students in mediation skills. She is a certified court mediator in New York and Massachusetts and a former associate with the law firm Orrick, Herrington & Sutcliffe LLP. The Nassau County Commission on Human Rights honored her with the Dr. Martin Luther King, Jr., Award in recognition of her innovative approach toward increasing tolerance and understanding among people by improving communication. Her name is inscribed on the Town of North Hempstead Women's Roll of Honor because of her many accomplishments. A highly respected speaker and lecturer, Puhn offers educational programs through the Laurie Puhn Institute. She lives in New York City. Her website address is www.lauriepuhn.com.

More Instant Persuasion

Laurie Puhn Communications
www.lauriepuhn.com
laurie@lauriepuhn.com
(516) 773-0303

✳ Become a member of the Instant Persuasion Club. Receive communication tips, Instant Persuasion event updates and notices of contests. Club membership is free.

✳ Share your communication tips and Instant Persuasion success stories. Visit www.lauriepuhn.com.

Keynote Presentations, Seminars and Workshops

The Laurie Puhn Institute offers programs that are customized for leadership training, businesspeople, physicians, lawyers, educators, students and personal growth audiences. Each Instant Persuasion program is uniquely crafted to educate, entertain and create a life-changing experience for participants.

Shop Online at the Instant Persuasion Store

To view and purchase Instant Persuasion products, visit www.lauriepuhn.com.